SPEAK,
MEMORABLY

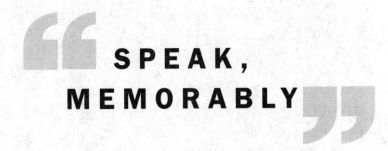

SPEAK, MEMORABLY

The Art of Captivating an Audience

BILL McGOWAN

AND JULIANA SILVA

HARPER
BUSINESS
An Imprint of HarperCollins*Publishers*

HarperCollins books may be purchased for educational, business, or sales promotional use. For information, please email the Special Markets Department at SPsales@harpercollins.com.

FIRST EDITION

Library of Congress Cataloging-in-Publication Data has been applied for.

ISBN 978-0-06-341519-5

25 26 27 28 29 LBC 5 4 3 2 1

To Vivian and Ana, two immensely quotable women.

Those who tell the stories rule the world.

—*Hopi American Indian proverb*

CONTENTS

INTRODUCTION

"Yes, I really do love how you're communicating with your eyes.
It's just what's coming out of your mouth that makes absolutely no sense."

In 2014, I wrote my first book, *Pitch Perfect: How to Say It Right the First Time, Every Time.* At the time, I thought it represented everything I wanted to say about being the very best communicator you could be in a variety of different life situations. I'm proud and thankful that it still does. But what a difference a decade can make! Today there are so many more scenarios to consider and sensitivities to respect.

At that time, Zoom was something you did when you floored the accelerator in your car. TikTok was the sound of an antique clock. AI? Isn't that the Stanley Kubrick/Steven Spielberg movie? Publicly saying outrageous things got you chastised and isolated, not idolized. That was before unhinged became the new authentic. Established institutions, like Ivy League universities, were rock-solid enough that they could shrug off the effects of a bad day of testimony from their leaders on Capitol Hill and return to their ivory towers unscathed. Today, an ill-conceived and poorly executed performance in front of the microphones and cameras can result in their very existence being questioned and their biggest donors hiding their checkbooks.

Years ago, many of us were unaware that the expressions "ladies and gentlemen" and "you guys" were living on borrowed time. We seemed to be a bit more tolerant of opposing viewpoints, a bit more patient while listening to others. Our culture had not yet fully devolved into a full-fledged shouting match between two echo chambers. That 24/7 dysfunctional din has escalated the noise level so high that to stand out and get noticed, some mistakenly think that establishing a distinctiveness requires cringe-worthy bad behavior.

This book is committed to steering us around that unseemly pothole in our communication, guiding us to an elevated and enduring stature that never goes out of style. Together we will explore the antidote to bland, boring, and forgettable. Attention that is based on cleverness and wisdom has a longer life span.

Today, being memorable is the holy grail of communication. At my company, we teach this every day to our clients, because if they've been coached before, typically they've been chasing a dusty and dated definition of success, one that is predicated on being messaged. The three edicts: come up with three key messages; keep bridging back to those messages; and tell 'em what you're going to tell 'em, tell 'em, and tell 'em what you told 'em.

Given all that has changed, it would seem to be an ideal time to offer a new set of ground rules for effective communication skills, especially at work, where they play a prominent role in determining our future success. These ground rules stress being memorable over just being messaged.

Here's why being memorable is a worthy aspiration. If you say something that rattles around in people's brains for a few hours, a few days, or longer, you've hit the communications jackpot. You are much more likely to persuade and influence others to see merit in your point of view. And so much of our professional communication is about getting buy-in and swaying people to adopt our point of view. But, before you can coax people to see eye-to-eye with you, you have to hook their attention and keep it, something that is hard to do given the forgettable communications scourge that permeates every level of the business world.

At work, a development that has been more of an insidious creep than a radical change is the proliferation of meetings. In a recent poll, 93 percent of U.S. workers identified meetings as the biggest bane of their professional existence. When asked what's wrong with meetings, 45 percent said they're too long, and 49 percent said that what gets communicated creates more confusion than clarity. Further complicating this is the lack of time we're given to fully digest and synthesize the purpose of the meeting, because frequently, when that meeting is over, we go right into the next. The density of meetings on our calendars can start to look like the arrivals board at JFK airport.

The chief saboteur of business meetings is the dry-as-a-bone, dull-as-dishwater, and maddeningly predictable slideshow presentation that the participants are subjected to, or as we commonly refer to it, "death by PowerPoint." It is the numbing sameness of these presentations that makes otherwise vibrant colleagues morph into petrified driftwood. I see this every day in my work as a communications coach. It's fairly common for professionals to loathe presenting to their colleagues, or worse, a roomful of strangers. This sets up a vicious cycle: the more you dislike presenting, the more likely you'll be to flatten out your content and delivery to "just get through it." In turn, the more you flatten out, the more your audience will tune out, and the less your narrative will connect and resonate.

In the following chapters, I will take you through a series of strategies and techniques designed to turn the vicious cycle into a flywheel of impact. Together we will dramatically change the definition of communication success, which in turn will unlock a bolder and more creative way of communicating that will captivate your audience.

PART I

COMMUNICO, ERGO SUM
(I COMMUNICATE, THEREFORE I AM)

In this section, we challenge the wisdom of the age-old expression "Talk is cheap." Together we will explore the infinite value of thoughtful and strategic self-expression. When we fully understand that, we enjoy more success, both personally and professionally. You will also be able to identify the unconscious ways we underestimate the power of our communication skills, which results in missed opportunities to achieve our full potential.

1

WHY MEMORABLE
COMMUNICATION MATTERS

"Can you start again? When you got to slide two, I started to wonder if I set the timer on my Instant Pot."

The business world has adopted the wrong definition of successful communication. For many years, being "on message" was considered the prime directive. But here's the problem with that: What's safe is usually not sticky. When everyone sounds messaged, no one stands out. Over the course of this book, you will be presented with a challenge to be memorable over merely being messaged. Regardless of where you work or where you are in your career, together we will discuss strategies to cut through the numbing sameness of boring business rhetoric that mutes our impact and dulls our personal brand. This challenge will require you to take a leap of faith and demonstrate a certain degree of courage. That's because the guidance in the pages that follow will implore you to go against what is professionally instinctive, and that is the need to fit in, and sometimes the bigger the organization, the more pressure we feel to assimilate. Try with all your grit and determination to resist that, because here's the troubling truth when it comes to our approach to communication at work: conformity makes you forgettable.

Think of what's most important when you're applying for a job you're itching to land—you want to distinguish yourself. Going for broke always eclipses playing it safe. Standing out and being remembered catapults you to the top of the consideration list. Now, imagine applying that same mindset to every day of your career, especially on those occasions when your communication skills play an outsize role in defining your professionalism. I maintain that every time you speak, whether it's a small meeting, an all-hands gathering, or a prospective client pitch, you are auditioning for the next prominent role that awaits you or the next account to be won. These are the moments in which you need to rise to the occasion and demonstrate your professional mettle.

Intimidating? Sure! Daunting? Absolutely! But then, exploring outside your comfort zone always is. But no greater risk-reward proposition exists. The promise that awaits you from taking this advice to heart is recognition, acknowledgment that you are not merely a product of some cookie-cutter corporate culture. By the end of this book, you will have the building blocks for captivating an audience. Key to that is knowing how to establish distinctiveness and clarity in presenting yourself in an original, authentic, and, most importantly, memorable way.

Improving our communication is widely regarded as the most important skill we can cultivate. In February 2024, LinkedIn published a report citing communication as the most in-demand skill for the second year in a row. According to the report, those who listed communication skills as one of their top skills in their LinkedIn profile were headhunted and hired more often. The report concluded that as a result of hybrid work, "employees communicate across an ever-expanding range of channels and platforms. Since in-person collaboration is no longer the default, effective communication from company and team leadership across channels helps connect, motivate, and inspire your teams." How we accomplish this in a virtual channel (Zoom, Teams, Meet, etc.) was an absolute *must* to address in this book, which is why you'll find an entire chapter dedicated to that later on.

I have devoted more than twenty years of my career to helping people sound distinctive in their verbal and nonverbal communication. The overwhelming majority of professionals today exist in a rigidly narrow range of empty business jargon. My coaching work helps them broaden that range and break the suffocating mold that is an overwhelming roadblock to their success, whether that's pitching their ideas with conviction, motivating their teams to stay focused and produce excellence, or clearly articulating the company mission and establishing the steps necessary to fulfill that mission. In a nutshell, our communication skills at work are a measure of how effective we are in transforming human potential into business results. Underestimating that, or overlooking it, is something we do at our own peril.

THE HONESTY BEHIND GREATNESS

I can almost always tell who is destined to be a great communicator. It's not the person who claims they're already very good and have no need to be coached. It is also not the person who listens to the coaching guidance with incessant, yeah-I-already-know-this head-nodding. When I encounter this, I don't skip ahead to the more advanced stuff. Instead I make sure I devote ample time to the basics, because I know a bluff when I see it.

It is extremely rare when that person's overconfident self-assessment is accurate. In fact, it's the cocky ones who are usually in most dire need of coaching. I always implore those people to "practice like you've never won and play like you've never lost." Recently, I worked with an executive who was poised to assume a new position as the head of his company's India region. It's a big promotion and vote of confidence for him, a daunting assignment in which he needs to rise to the occasion and wow all the people who will soon be reporting to him. I left the session with him 100 percent convinced that he would be a smashing success, an appraisal based on one thing he said to me: "If you give me a training regimen that I can follow after this session, I will do it. It doesn't matter if it takes two hours a day, three hours a day, I will do it." I would be willing to bet the bank that there's no way this guy is going to come up short.

THE BIGGER THEY ARE, THE HARDER THEY WORK

I wish this were true of all celebrities and titans of industry. Sometimes ego gets in the way of acknowledging that they're not perfect and that help is needed. But thankfully, in my experience, the ones who are bound for greatness, or are already great, are relentless learners and have an inner sense of security that opens the door to feedback and coaching. Such was the case with Kim Kardashian.

When she descended a staircase in her Calabasas, California, home, Kim's makeup and hair were perfect. Comfortably attired in a bathrobe, she claimed that she really needed the training session we were about to do. I thought the opposite might be true: that she was underestimating herself. After all, few people have spent a greater percentage of their adult waking moments in front of a camera than Kim Kardashian. She feels as comfortable in the glare of the spotlight as we do sitting in our kitchens with a morning cup of coffee. So frankly, I was more than a bit surprised when she requested a coaching session. Her goal was not to have quicker one-liners in episodes of *Keeping Up with the Kardashians*. On this occasion, she was scheduled to be interviewed by Steve Forbes, onstage at the Forbes Women's Summit. The subject was not going to be in her customary wheelhouse of trendsetting. Instead, Forbes wanted to delve into Kim Kardashian the entrepreneur, the savvy businesswoman, who was opportunistically diversifying and expanding beyond her pop culture celebrity status.

I knew we were off to a good start when she pulled out a black Moleskin notebook and started taking detailed notes. Her phone was not touched for three hours. That's like a hedge fund trader not looking at their Bloomberg Box for the entire afternoon.

That session led to a full-blown training for her entire family that they filmed as an episode of their show *Keeping Up with the Kardashians*. Every member of the family was incredibly professional. They recognized this exercise as one more piece in the elaborate puzzle that determines to what extent they will be able to control their own narrative.

One area the Kardashians did *not* need help with was the ability to be engaging and memorable. But for those of us who are not followed by tens of millions of fans on social media, the quest to keep people's attention when we speak can be a challenging one. Communication in the workplace often comes down to one primary goal: being persuasive. Perhaps we're trying to get that big promotion, pitch new business with prospective clients, convince others to invest their money with us, or inspire and motivate employees to all execute a new strategy. If our communication skills fail to achieve engagement and retention, then the quest to persuade becomes a moot point and our efforts amount to nothing more than wasted breath.

For most of us, the lion's share of our communication opportunities occurs in meetings, notoriously where effective communication goes to die. In fact, if you told a group of people that they could change one thing about their work culture, the unanimous response would likely be "fewer long, boring meetings." *meetings*

In a research study conducted by the productivity software company Atlassian, the number one barrier to productivity in most workplaces was meetings, with 72 percent of them labeled as "ineffective." How discouraging to realize that when you look at your calendar, three out of every four meetings you have scheduled will be regarded as a waste of time and resources.

Jack Dorsey, the CEO of the technology company Block, declared Tuesdays a meeting-free day in the hopes of fostering more productivity. More and more companies are following Dorsey's lead as they recognize that they have a serious productivity crisis on their hands. Many are coming to the frightening awareness that the sole outcome of most meetings is the determination that another meeting is necessary. That's the problematic epiphany Amazon came to in the third quarter of 2024. CEO Andy Jassy sent a letter to everyone in the organization declaring that Amazon has evolved into a lumbering bureaucracy. To prove the point, he called out a company-wide propensity for scheduling "premeetings for the pre-meetings for the decision meetings."

Meeting fatigue is real and not just due to the quantity of meetings. Even if your calendar shows just a few meetings, often they are sprinkled throughout the day in such a way that getting any real quality work done is impossible.

What often makes those meetings so tedious are the dreaded presentations that drag on and on and waste precious time, aka "death by PowerPoint." Since reducing the number of meetings in most corporate cultures will take nothing short of a Herculean effort, there's only one solution: make the quality of the meetings better. If we make the ones we are required to attend more engaging, clearer, and more concise in the message we're sending, we make them more memorable and attain lasting impact.

In a recent LinkedIn poll, people were asked to identify the biggest turnoff when it comes to presentations. Nineteen percent cited poor content, 14 percent said poor audience interaction, 5 percent said poor slides, and a whopping 63 percent said poor delivery.

Imagine the possibilities if we upped our game in articulating our thoughts. Greater proficiency in delivery could lead to an increase in two of the most precious commodities in our professional lives: time and productivity. Across entire companies, help in this area has never been more needed. That was the conclusion drawn in 2023 when the tech communications company Grammarly teamed up with the Harris

Poll company to get a handle on just how much damage is caused by poor communication within companies. The numbers are staggering. Poor communication was cited as the reason for $1.2 trillion of losses each year—yes, that's trillion with a t. In their study, all the key indicators were shown to be heading in the wrong direction.

The perceived effectiveness of communication by business leaders dropped 12 percent, a decrease exacerbated by a 9 percent increase in the number of hours knowledge workers spend communicating each week. So, at the very time we are communicating more, the quality we're bringing to it is precipitously dropping. It's no wonder that the number of business leaders who reported a decrease in productivity directly attributable to poor communications climbed by 15 percent.

That's why the intent of this book goes far beyond merely transforming you into a better, more memorable communicator, although that's a worthy enough cause in and of itself. Better yet, I want you to emerge from this read with the capacity to be a communications role model, an ambassador for a new and engaging approach to public speaking. That may sound like an overly ambitious goal, but it's not. It is the flip side of the learn-through-osmosis phenomenon. Decades ago, professionals learned how to communicate in a bland, dull, and forgettable way by listening and learning from that era's ambassadors of drab, the jargon jerks. It has been cemented into place because the leaders of tomorrow emulated the speaking style of executives they reported to, mistakenly thinking that's the language that leads to success. Time to flip the osmosis coin over. Now, armed with a new way of thinking, I have every confidence that you'll be fully equipped to be a modern-day Pied Piper of effective communication. Consider this an invitation to join a movement that compels us to express ourselves in the most human way possible, unfettered by the pressures to conform to an antiquated style that lumps everyone together into an indistinguishable mass.

I guarantee you that with each chapter, you will discover techniques that are holding you back from realizing your full potential as a communicator and say, "OMG! I do that! I think I've always done that, and how is it that no one's ever told me I shouldn't be doing that?" I'm confident that will be a recurring revelation because that's exactly what clients tell me at some point in every one-on-one coaching session.

THE GOOD RIPPLE EFFECT

The benefits of adopting a more engaging and memorable way of communicating yields benefits at work that extend beyond others modeling your public-speaking behavior. Clear and effective communication can enhance collaboration, and conversely, poor communication can bring teamwork to a grinding halt. According to the *Harvard Business Review*, 85 percent or more of a typical employee's workweek is spent in collaboration mode. That's a 50 percent increase over the last ten years. If you consider that in tandem with the results of a Salesforce survey that found that 86 percent of executives and employees say that lack of team communication skills causes failed projects (and effective communication increases team productivity by 25 percent), it paints a vivid picture of how direct a link there is between business success and clear and effective communication.

These numbers reflect what I have experienced firsthand in my role as the head of a communications coaching firm for the past twenty-three years. Back in the early 2000s, it was mainly the media and lifestyle brands that placed a premium on these skills. Today companies in virtually every industry, from tech to banking, from insurance to professional sports, from health care to automobile makers, recognize that their drivers of growth are no longer confined to just factors like product-market fit and innovation. Their P&L is directly impacted by how effectively their people communicate both internally and externally.

To gauge the accuracy of this observation, and many others in the chapters that follow, we commissioned a survey by Clarity Media Group of over one hundred people. The respondent pool was comprised of full- and part-time employees between the ages of twenty-five and sixty-five. With regard to the question of how important public-speaking skills are to work, nearly 40 percent said they constantly work on improving their presentation skills because they see that ability as crucial to their career advancement. Less than 14 percent thought they were not important.

DO YOU CONSIDER YOUR PUBLIC-SPEAKING SKILLS AT WORK IMPORTANT?

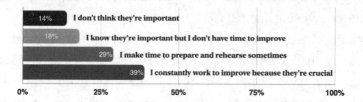

To assign an even higher level of importance to public-speaking skills, a growing number of business leaders see the skillful communication of their message as critical to their company's overall performance. This reality became crystal-clear to me several years ago when I was driving down the 101 freeway between San Francisco and Palo Alto. I was listening to an interview with Aaron Levie, the founder and CEO of the cloud storage company Box. The interviewer asked Levie why he thought his company's IPO had underperformed in light of loftier industry expectations. I found his response fascinating. Instead of suggesting that the fault lay with the investment bank leading the offering, or an inaccurate valuation of his company, or even poor market timing, he said, "The performance was the result of never coming up with a narrative that fit on the back of a cocktail napkin."

Until that moment, even I thought that being a great communicator with a compelling narrative was merely a business bonus, a nice thing to have. But the Levie interview changed my perception. Today skillful communication is a business imperative, a reality that is not lost on public companies who see their stock performance affected by their word selection and their tone of voice on earnings calls.

The scripts that the CEO and CFO read from are always thoroughly vetted by the legal, compliance, and communications experts within the company. But when we work from these scripts in training sessions, rarely are they sufficiently accentuating the positive and contextualizing the negative. This can have two unfortunate outcomes: either the company's performance is perceived as worse than the reality, or the leadership team's attempt to project optimism amid systemic problems fails to be convincing and falls flat.

Increasingly, the decision as to whether executives are rewarded or punished for their communication performances rests with technology. Many of today's analysts and fund managers rely on a tool called natural language processing (NLP) to analyze an executive's true state of mind. NLP uses algorithms to study word selection to discover revealing and accurate signals on how the company is really doing. If words like "issues" or "challenges" come up frequently, that tells you something about a company's current and future prospects. It's a tool fund managers use in the hopes of neutralizing the efforts of investor relations teams who are skilled at wordsmithing corporate results to create an overly rosy picture.

However, a 2023 article in the *Financial Times* revealed that as helpful as transcripts are, companies were manipulating semantics to their advantage. "We found tremendous value from transcripts," said Yin Luo, head of quantitative research at Wolfe Research. "The problem that has created for us and many others is that overall sentiment is becoming more and more positive . . . [because] company management knows their messages are being analyzed."

In this mano-a-mano battle, analysts have now turned to AI to regain the upper hand. Firms are now looking at not just word selection but how the words are spoken. In the *FT*'s reporting, investment funds are now favoring the combination of NLP and audio recordings of earnings calls to decipher the true performance prospects of any company. The recordings provide insights that transcripts alone cannot, like the sound of uncertainty in an exec's voice or the use of filler words that increase when a person is anxious and under pressure. According to the *FT*, artificial intelligence can also detect "microtremors" in a person's voice, which are imperceptible to the human ear.

This brave-new-world scenario has already claimed a victim.

Francis deSouza was the CEO of a company called Illumina. At the time of one of his earnings calls, deSouza was grilled by investors as to how a controversy surrounding his contentious takeover of another company was affecting Illumina's outlook. On paper, deSouza seemed to say the right thing, that the drama "was affecting only a small part of the company." But when his comments were processed by a voice analytics firm using AI, an interesting pattern was discovered. Each time he had to respond to questions about the troubled takeover, the pitch and the pace of his voice deviated from his typical delivery and he resorted to using more filler words than normal.

The analysis concluded that the changes in speech patterns indicated greater stress and anxiety over the takeover topic. Two months later, deSouza was gone.

AI's ability to see through a script that is framed through a positive lens has proven to be highly effective, except with one group: actors. That's because actors have the ability to convincingly project a mood and an attitude behind the words that AI has not been able to differentiate from legitimate emotions, at least not yet.

All of this underscores a piece of advice I offer to all clients I coach: public speaking is a performance, and it must be approached in that light. For many of us, projecting and emoting in a way that feels a little over-the-top is probably just about right. It's all about helping people see how they communicate through a different lens, the lens through which others see you instead of the one through which you see yourself. Those two lenses are calibrated completely differently. Until people watch themselves on video—without a doubt, *the* most dreaded exercise—they don't realize how underwhelming they come across. They think that on a scale of 1–10, they're a solid 8, but in truth, rating them as a 4 would be overly generous. In fact, when clients see the video of their rehearsal, frequently their overriding reaction is, "I had no idea how lifeless I seem. I thought I was really bringing it!"

PREPARATION FOSTERS CALM

What separates one of your best presentations from one of your worst may simply be a product of preparation. People tell me all the time that when they take the time to prepare, they are less nervous and perform better. But the difference between a good day and a bad day often is not very dramatic. Our performances exist in a fairly narrow range. Expanding that range so that your good days bring spectacular outcomes is a matter of thinking differently. Adopting a different mindset is the only way to achieve sustainable change. It's not a matter of drawing up a long list of what not to do. Curating a select set of powerfully effective strategies for what works and what gets remembered is the key. For me and my colleagues, the ultimate achievement is not having people say, "You've changed the way I speak." It's much more rewarding to have them say, "You've changed the way I think about speaking." It's not unlike how any nutritionist would advise you on eating healthier. Following a two-week regimen that resembles a structured diet rarely succeeds. But if you can change your awareness, attitude, and approach to food, the chances for longer-term success are much greater.

After reading this book, I suspect you will watch others present in a very different way. It's very likely you'll be a much more informed and insightful observer of other people's public-speaking techniques. Up until now, you probably made a general assessment that someone was either captivating or tedious to listen to. But now each presentation you are required to sit through presents an opportunity to analyze the speaker in a detailed way, with a newfound awareness of what techniques on display are working, and which aren't. This is how to cement the learnings from this book and increase the likelihood of pulling off your own communication transformation.

Then, once armed with an effective new sense of awareness and a fresh game plan, improvement can result from a few different tactics. In our Clarity survey, we wanted to get a sense of what proactive steps people were taking. We presented four options: asking colleagues for feedback, watching online videos of good speakers, working with a professional coach, and all of the above. Over 40 percent selected the lowest-impact and least-effective method of asking for feedback. This would not be my recommendation for a couple of reasons. One, those whom you're asking to rate you may not have a clue what makes for good presentation skills. And two, everybody lies when they're asked, "How did I do?" "Oh, you were great!" is the most common response, the least truthful and also the least valuable. You can still ask people immediately afterward if you crave the instant feedback. Just don't place too much stock in the replies.

The other three survey selections represent a much more constructive approach.

IF IMPROVING YOUR PUBLIC-SPEAKING SKILLS IS IMPORTANT TO YOU, WHAT STEPS HAVE YOU TAKEN TO GET BETTER?

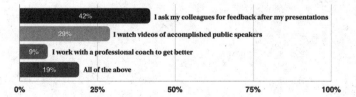

Bravo to the nearly 20 percent who took a multipronged approach to improving, which is what is likely to move the needle in the most meaningful and efficient way.

In the pages that follow, I want you to be confident that profound changes in the way you communicate are not only possible, but likely, if you commit to venturing outside your comfort zone. Together we will experiment with new techniques that offer the best opportunity to achieve the ultimate goal: to be distinctive in how you communicate and to speak memorably.

SAY THIS	NOT THAT
"Among all our partners . . ."	"All across the entire value chain . . ."
"Responding to all our consumers' needs."	"Meeting consumers wherever they are . . ."
"Helping employees maximize their potential."	"Supporting employees in their upskilling journey."
"Let's examine this more closely . . ."	"Let's double-click on this . . ."

PART II

THE SHORT-WINDED
RACONTEUR

In this section, we will dispel one of the great myths about public speaking, that storytelling skills and brevity are mutually exclusive. The next two chapters will illustrate how storytelling does not require that you spin a long yarn. It *does* require that you conjure up visual images in the minds of your audience, utilizing an economy of words.

2

THE COPPOLA
STORYTELLING FORMULA

"I don't really have three dynamic points to make. Would five forgettable ones suffice?"

In 2022, I watched an interview on CNN with the legendary Holly-wood film director Francis Ford Coppola, whose vast screen accomplishments include *The Godfather*, a movie many consider the greatest of all time. So, when Coppola agrees to sit down and discuss his views on storytelling, I drop everything and listen with rapt attention.

Fareed Zakaria, host of the CNN special series *Extraordinary*, asked him if he had a formula for making movies.

Look and decide what's the best thing you have, the second-best thing, and the third-best thing. Take the best thing you have and make it the ending of the movie, and take the second-best thing and make it the beginning of the movie and the third thing put in between those two.

I always thought [that] was really clever because of course what you see at the beginning of the movie you want to win the audience to you in that first scene, but that's not as important as what you want to do at the end of the movie when you want to have them leave with something wonderful because then they'll tell all their friends to go see the movie.

Coppola was talking about storytelling, but that strategy applies to many fields of endeavor. One of America's most revered chefs and celebrated restaurateurs (The French Laundry, Per Se, Bouchon), Thomas Keller, firmly believes that "the most important moments of the meal are the first five minutes and the last five minutes."

When you leave a Broadway musical, odds are the melody you'll be humming or lyrics you'll be singing are from the high-energy closing number, the last part of which is called the coda. David Yazbek, a Tony Award–winning composer, says starting off with a bang is important, but how you conclude matters every bit as much.

"The coda is what sticks with people, what they will remember, and what will trigger their memories of what's been communicated in the piece."

This concept has been validated in organizational psychology studies that show that a key reason why audiences retain information has to do with where you position the information. Nineteenth-century psychologist Hermann Ebbinghaus conducted experiments on memory and concluded that information presented at the beginning and end of a learning episode tends to be retained better than information presented in the middle. This is called the primacy/recency effect, a theory that, if it had been presented to Coppola, would have been "an offer he couldn't" refute, as the Godfather, Don Corleone, might have said.

This primacy/recency effect is a mindset you should always embrace when you are preparing to give a speech or presentation. Starting with a punch and ending with a bang is essential packaging for any form of communication. In 2024, when President Joe Biden badly stumbled verbally in the first debate of the presidential campaign, perhaps his most notable deficiency was his inability to finish his thoughts and complete his sentences. You can dazzle audiences with the most poignant and articulate thought, but if the wheels come off in the homestretch of your point and you career wildly across the finish line, that's all people are going to remember. Your earlier gem is now just a worthless stone.

Research into the recency effect suggests that retention of information is strongest with regard to the last thing you say. The primacy effect tends to be strongest when it comes to making value judgments about the speaker, not the least of which is "Do I like this person?"

Considering the importance of the start and the finish, we were curious how many people devote time to meticulously planning both, whether that's the beginning and end of the entire presentation, or the top and bottom you give to each and every slide in your deck. In our survey, more people responded "never" or "rarely" than replied "frequently."

HOW OFTEN DO YOU KNOW WITH CERTAINTY THE FIRST AND LAST SENTENCE OF EACH SLIDE?

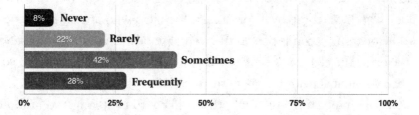

STUMBLING OUT OF THE STARTING BLOCKS

Failing to grab the attention of your audience from word one is bad enough, but doing something to irritate or alienate them is ten times worse. My pet peeve is when a keynote speaker at an event comes onstage and energetically says "good morning" to the crowd, only to get in return what they consider an unacceptably lukewarm response. That inevitably prompts the playfully intended, yet grotesquely ill-advised scolding of the audience: "Hey, c'mon! Is that the best you can do? Jeez! Let's try that again. I said, GOOD MORNING, EVERYONE!"

If I'm in the audience at that moment, there are three things running through my mind:

1. Is this clown really going to make me repeat myself because their ego was bruised?
2. Are they really so insecure that they need me to scream salutations back at them?
3. I really bristle when people tell me I'm insufficient in some way.

Boy, talk about getting off to a bad start! There's that old adage rearing its ugly head again about there being no second chances to make a first impression, so don't blow it! Trying to persuade or influence an audience to adopt your point of view after you've admonished them for not showering you with sufficient enthusiasm is a pretty steep climb. The enthusiasm you show in greeting the audience in the first few seconds should resemble the warmth you display greeting close friends at the front door who have come over for dinner. Speakers who appear off-putting in the opening seconds poison the well of goodwill with their audience and forfeit the chance to captivate them. Your audience's reaction to you when you first appear in front of them will likely be either "Hmmm, this should be interesting" or "Ooh, this is likely to be a long and arduous affair." Once that impression is set, it can be hard to change it.

PRESENTERS' MOST OVERUSED WORD

Let's also agree to hit the abort button on a couple of other launch items that are tired old clichés. If you can get through your first thirty seconds without telling the audience how "excited" you are, you gain admittance into an elite community of communication one-percenters. The word "excited" is suffering from intense exhaustion. It has been said to death, and as a result it is a terrible way to use your first several seconds to sound distinctive. We live in a show-don't-tell world, in which demonstrating your excitement is far more powerful than declaring your excitement. Just be careful not to let those demonstrations go so over-the-top that you look like a complete lunatic, as former Microsoft CEO Steve Ballmer did in 2011. Ballmer came onstage at a Microsoft company meeting, running around the stage, screaming like an eight-year-old on a roller coaster for nearly a minute. The first time I saw it, I thought an army of red ants had invaded his trousers. I'm sure some of the Microsoft faithful loved it, but when a sizable portion of your audience asks themselves in unison, "Has this dude TOTALLY lost his mind?" it's probably time to scale back the craziness.

NO TIME IS A GOOD TIME

Another threadbare technique that should be strictly forbidden is the overused apology for your time slot. It doesn't matter if you're scheduled to speak first thing in the morning or the last part of the day: people are convinced their spot in the order is the worst. The person onstage at 9 a.m. apologizes: "Now, I know many of you were out late last night . . . I see a few bleary eyes. So I'll try to be brief."

The speaker at 11 a.m. apologizes: "I'm sure some of you are already starting to daydream about what's for lunch and you're probably getting hungry, but stay with me here . . ."

The presenter after lunch apologizes: "I'm sure a lot of you are feeling a little of that after-lunch lethargy. You're probably thinking a little nap would be nice right about now . . ."

And the speaker at 4 p.m. has the most predictable clichéd apology of them all: "Now, listen . . . I know I'm the only thing standing between you and the cocktail hour, but we have a few items we need to get through."

There's only one time I ever suggested in a training session that someone actually use that 4 p.m. apology. It was a spirits convention in which a mixologist was asked to demonstrate a number of mixed cocktails as the close to a day of presentations. Members of the audience were given the chance to sample some of them, which inspired us to have the mixologist say, "I can't really say that I'm the only thing standing between you and the cocktail hour, simply because I *am* the cocktail hour." Anytime you have the opportunity to play around with an overused expression, go for it!

DON'T SKIP THE BULLPEN

Many people have told me over the years that they get significantly better once they're warmed up, three or four slides into the presentation. To that I say, like a pitcher in baseball, you need to warm up. Find a quiet place at the venue to say the first five minutes of your speech or presentation out loud. Struggling to find your rhythm during slides one and two is a surefire way to lose your audience, especially in light of the disproportionate importance the beginning holds. A host of different data exists on the amount of time you have when you begin to speak to make a first impression. In an unforgivingly brief period of time, your audience will have made a determination whether they like you and if they want to connect with what you're saying.

The audience sensing redundancy from the speaker is never a good thing, but it's particularly bad in the first thirty seconds, which is when many presenters are guilty of it. This is the "intro redo" phenomenon, in which the speaker begins their presentation by introducing themselves (name, job title, responsibilities), a totally unnecessary step when the previous speaker took care of those details for you when they invited you to the microphone. But even if no one introduced you, it would still be a more dynamic beginning if you launched into a brief story and then you revealed to the audience who you are after the payoff to the story. Many people initially bristle at this coaching suggestion, fearing that the audience is going to be left wondering who the speaker is during this story. That's totally fine! That momentary bewilderment is a form of engagement, plus the story is going to be far more captivating than the robotic delivery of name, rank, and serial number.

SNAP JUDGMENTS

Avoiding a ho-hum routine start is crucial because studies show that your audience is deciding whether they like what you have to offer in the first seven seconds.

Behavioral scientist Vanessa Van Edwards enlisted 760 volunteers to rate two groups of speakers based on their first impressions. One group got to see only seven-second clips, the other group saw the complete lectures. The results were remarkable. The top-rated presentations were the ones that were given the highest marks within the first seven seconds, even when audio was absent. The key takeaway? Audiences know good presenters when they first see them, so presenters have no time to waste.

RELEASE YOUR AGENDA

Even if you've successfully navigated this opening-minute minefield, be afraid—very afraid! For there's one big, hulking engagement-killer lurking out there. It has claimed many victims in the world of corporate presentations and its reign of tedium and boredom seems to continue unabated. I'm referring to the dreaded "agenda slide," two words that should spark a sense of dread in the hearts and minds of every audience member. "Isn't it a good thing to set the audience's expectation on what you'll be speaking about?" you ask. To that my response is, "When was the last time you bought a book with an insatiable desire to bring it home and dive into the table of contents?" My guess is, never!

Setting the agenda gets your presentation off to a grinding halt. In fact, anything that leads you to talk about what you're going to talk about is precious time taken away from just talking about it. You would be amazed how much time you can trim off your presentation by not warning people about what you're going to do next. From this point on, I'd like you to adhere to the mantra "Inform, don't warn." The warnings come in several different forms: "To illustrate that point, let me share with you a story." Not necessary! Just launch into the story. "To prove that thesis, I'd like to draw your attention to this data point." Wasted breath! Just share the statistic.

To captivate an audience and be memorable, I urge you to adjust the big-picture way you think about your presentation. Most people mistakenly treat the overall presentation as merely a series of isolated and disconnected slides that address the topics they need to cover. Your results will be much better if you view it through a different lens, one that challenges you to identify the overarching story you're telling. Why? Because stories are memorable. Stories help us grab the gist of an idea quickly. They trigger our emotions. Folding key information inside anecdotes is like hiding broccoli florets in your children's pasta dish. It makes it more appealing and it sticks to their ribs. Those were the findings of cognitive psychologist Jerome Bruner, who suggests we are twenty-two times more likely to remember a fact when it has been wrapped in a story.

In Chapter 5, we will look at the effectiveness of what we call "jumbo analogies" as a starting point for a speech or presentation. Think of that device as a metaphorical thread you weave through your content. Most people introduce the analogous story, deliver it, and drop it. But when you're able to make it a recurring theme that pops back up a couple of times, your remarks take on a polished, well-produced quality. The people in our survey who approached their presentation merely as a collection of slides, rather than as a story that holds together, with a discernible beginning, middle, and end, outnumbered (albeit slightly) those who saw it as a yarn they were weaving and bringing people along on a narrative ride.

THE PRESENTATION CHASM

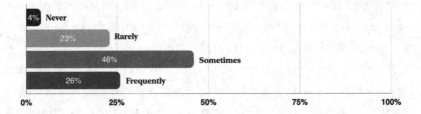

WHEN YOU PUT A PRESENTATION TOGETHER HOW OFTEN DO YOU THINK OF IT AS A STORY YOU'RE TELLING?

Given that the opening seconds are so crucial to a memorable presentation, I typically spend twice as long with clients crafting the content they start with than I do with anything else that follows before the close. Ironically, the opening seconds are when people fall back on winging it the most, saying whatever pops into their heads. It doesn't make any sense to be at your most uncertain and roughest at the very time when the audience is judging you the harshest.

Let's accept the fact that you will probably need to thank one or two people when you first begin, and then express your gratitude or enthusiasm for the opportunity to speak. Let's call this section the "pleasantries." Some people have a general idea of how this will roll off their tongue, but most try to do it on autopilot, which is why you hear "I'm so excited to be here" all the time. Then there's the actual "presentation," which begins with your presenter's notes for slide one. But in nearly every presentation I've either heard or worked on, there is roughly a thirty-second gap between the pleasantries and the presentation, which

I call the "presentation chasm," where the mouth goes rogue and is disengaged from any intentional or strategic narrative. The lack of certainty over where you're going leads to overtalking, which creates a random, haphazard feel to the presentation. The inevitable outcome? You're forced to utter the cringey, awkward non sequitur "All right, so I guess we'll get started." When you say that, you have taken a perilous plunge headfirst into the presentation chasm.

To avoid that public-speaking death dive, you need to meticulously build a thematically smooth bridge that spans the chasm from pleasantries to presentation. In many of my own presentations, this is where my biggest investment of time is focused. To gain a clear picture of what goes into these bridges, let me take you through the construction process of one I had to recently build.

Together with my Clarity colleagues Juliana Silva (contributor to this book as well) and Bill Cassara, I was invited to a client's off-site meeting in Austin, Texas. Our job was to help the thirty comms professionals in attendance advance their skills in prepping their own executives for media interviews. They graciously invited us to arrive the day before our training so we could join them all for dinner. Most of them were like us, former journalists who know the tricks of the trade that reporters use to conduct media interviews. They had been briefed on the purpose of our visit. After we presented media-training strategy to them, they would break off into groups and subject themselves to some hardball practice media interviews at our hands.

At dinner the night before, everyone was warm and gracious to us, but many of them hadn't seen one another since before the pandemic, so in their eagerness to reconnect and catch up, they clustered together for dinner. Not feeling the slightest bit slighted, Juliana, Bill, and I kept each other company at a separate table.

Later that night, as I was putting some finishing touches on the presentation I had to give the following morning, a vast chasm was staring me in the face. I knew I'd have to begin with some mention of dinner the night before, but the first slide of my deck was a quote from George

Orwell that says, "Journalism is printing what someone else doesn't want printed. Everything else is public relations." Talk about a daunting abyss! Worse yet, I really wanted to inject some humor, as we will fully explore in Chapter 4. This bridge would need five separate spans to get from one side to the other:

Span 1: "It was really a rare treat for us to be able to get to know many of you at dinner last night. Normally, we don't arrive early enough to have that opportunity."

Span 2: "I must say, though, I did detect a certain amount of wariness on the part of some of you. I think you were aware of what you were walking into here this morning, an exercise where you'd be put in the hot seat and tested under aggressive questioning."

Span 3: "I was half-expecting some of you might be looking to slip me a hundred-dollar bill under the table as an incentive—or should I say bribe—to go easy on you."

Span 4: "But I get it. The majority of you are ex-journalists. You know full well what can happen to someone in the interview chair."

Span 5 connected directly to the narrative of slide one: "You probably subscribe to what I call the George Orwell Theory, that reporters are paid to poke holes in people's narratives, not amplify their narratives."

Each one of these bridge spans represents a segue, a meticulous stitching of connective tissue of content that ties together various storytelling elements to make a cohesive story. That is what you're constantly doing in speeches and presentations, hopefully with enough finesse that the audience never sees the stitch marks. With that goal in mind, I'm constantly bewildered by presenters who go out of their way to call attention to their non sequiturs: "Okay, so let's shift gears and talk about something different," or, "Now I want to pivot for a minute and spend a little time discussing . . ." Remember, "Inform, don't warn." You may think that warning is necessary, but I can tell you with certainty that there's never been a case in which a smooth, segued transition wasn't a viable option over an abrupt and clumsy thematic turn.

The importance of subtlety in transitions holds true not just with the broad overarching story you're telling, but also on a micro level in terms of each individual slide. Whether the scale of the storytelling is grand or granular, the Coppola Formula remains in effect.

Within each slide, I want you to plan and thoroughly rehearse three things:

1. The opening line that gets you into the slide
2. The big takeaway from the slide—the sticky idea
3. The last line of the slide or the segue line that foreshadows the next slide

Each one of these should be a punchy, concise, and declarative statement, not a long windup to what you'll be thematically addressing in the slide.

Working off a script you've memorized verbatim is not an option. Even if you have a photographic memory and there's zero chance of you losing your way, I still urge you not to do it. That's because the more memorized your content, the flatter and more robotic you will sound delivering it. There are only three lines to know by heart. Everything else can be reduced to sparse bullet points that you talk through. This strategy will force you to be in thinking mode instead of reciting mode, which will make you sound more thoughtful and more conversational.

THE OPENING LINE

Too often, presenters throw away a golden opportunity within a presentation to dictate to the audience how they should think. That opportunity is available in the very first sentence you say after you hit the clicker to change the slide. Think of that line as a lens setter. In your opening line you are persuading and influencing the audience to absorb the ensuing information the way you want them to. So, instead of the traditional start—"Now, if we look at this performance in the context of a global perspective"—eliminate the windup and get straight to flexing your powers of persuasion muscle: "Internationally, we exceeded the performance we expected." Whatever you say from this point on will be filtered through the lens of success. The shorter and punchier the lead sentence, the less drag you'll bring to your pacing. When a speech or presentation feels as though it lacks vitality, it's rarely the result of vocal pacing, and it's almost always the result of just simply too much content. You can speak a million miles an hour, but if you don't bring a minimalist approach to your content, it won't be long before you see people start to fidget in their seats.

THE TAKEAWAY

Within each slide, ask yourself, "What's the most important idea I'm conveying? What do I want the audience remembering above all other information I provide in this slide?" After you identify it, express it in the punchiest and most concise way possible. To make it stand out even more, you can also "drumroll up to it." By that I mean precede the big idea with a setup phrase we call a "drumroll line." An example of that could be "Success for us boils down to one basic premise." Then build in a slight pause to heighten a little sense of anticipation for the payoff to the drumroll line, which could be "The more diverse our portfolio, the less susceptible we are to a softening market." By phrasing this last line with "more" and "less," we've structured the payoff like a mathematical equation/ratio. This is a memorable way to frame your ideas, which we will discuss further in Chapter 5. Another example of a drumroll/payoff: "For us, a winning formula comes down to this: the more consumer demands change, the more agile we need to be."

If you can have a slide accompanying the payoff to the drumroll that has merely an arresting image or a single number or lone word, that would heighten the memorable impact. In the book *Brain Rules*, author John Medina cites studies reporting that retention rates leap from 10 percent to a whopping 65 percent when pictures are used over text.

One of the greatest tactical benefits of the drumroll line is its ability to grab the attention of the audience in advance of delivering the big idea. Let's be honest. No matter how great an orator you are, you're always going to get drift from your audience. It's only natural for people to momentarily zone out and start fantasizing about what they're going to have for lunch. That means we, as public speakers, are in the drift-killing business, and the best time to put an end to their drift is right before your key takeaway thought. Despite their reverie, the ear of the audience is still engaged with you, even if not fully. So when your drumroll line promises a payoff to a crucial setup question, in that instant, the attention of the audience returns out of curiosity to hear the payoff. Like any technique, it's best not to overdose on it. Use it somewhat sparingly and you'll find less audience daydreaming at the most critical moments of your talk.

THE FINISH LINE

If you subscribe to the Coppola Formula and the recency effect, then the last thing you say in each slide is the most important. The problem is that most people come to a gradual, coasting stop at the end of a slide, as if they've run out of content gas. A crisp, punchy synopsis of the main point of the slide works well, as does a transition or segue line that foreshadows and teases what's coming up on the next slide. These transitions are crucial to create the feel of a flowing narrative.

Let's say you're a retail fashion company, and you're giving a presentation on sales performance for the recently completed quarter. Slide five of your deck details sales figures for your Chicago flagship store. Slide six shows the level of sales activity in your satellite stores around the country. The instinct of most presenters would be to conclude slide five by saying, "So, that gives you a sense of how our flagship store did . . ." Then they click to slide six and resume: "Now, if we look at performance from a satellite-store perspective, here's the picture that emerges." There are a lot of wasted words in that approach. Instead I suggest you hint at slide six before you click to it. To wrap up slide five, perhaps the segue line could be "As strong as our performance was at our flagship store, sales were even more robust at our satellite stores." Now you click to advance to slide six, saying, "Regardless of what region you look at, we crushed it." In your deck, the slide after that, slide seven, is about new inventory, so when you wrap up the narrative of slide six, the transition line could be "From our analysis, it's clear that one major factor was responsible for this boost of sales, [click to advance] our new inventory clicked with consumers." Here the drumroll line comes at the end as a way to tease and segue to the following slide, proving that a good drumroll works anywhere.

Foreshadowing what's to come is a device fiction writers often use at the end of a chapter and playwrights weave into the end of an act in theater. It piques your curiosity over what happens next and keeps engagement high. But for some reason, people don't take advantage of this technique when presenting their deck. That's why it's important to change your whole mindset about making a presentation. It's not about building fifteen stand-alone slides—it's about seeing what you have to say as a cohesive story, with a beginning, middle, and end that should take the audience on a flowing, narrative ride. It doesn't matter how scintillating or mundane the subject matter. My guess is that if Francis Ford Coppola were a midlevel manager at a manufacturing company who had to put together a presentation on the effects of supply-chain disruptions on the company's ability to meet its manufacturing quota, he would still find a way to make that narrative capture your attention from the opening line all the way to the end.

The added bonus to deploying this strategy is that you will make your presentations punchier and leaner, and when you exercise brevity, your audience remembers more of what you say, something we will explore in the next chapter.

DO THIS	NOT THAT
Inform Your Audience	Warn Them What's Coming Next
Lead with a Declarative Statement	Talk About What You're Going to Talk About
Finish with a Bang	Gradually Taper Off at the End
Present Your Deck as a Cohesive Story	Treat Your Deck as a Collection of Disconnected Slides

3

THE VERBAL DIET

*"I'd like to see you get down to 12,000 words a day,
so remember, no chit-chatting between meals."*

For a Wednesday night, the restaurant on Avery Row in London was crowded. At the table directly to our left was Kevin Dillon of *Entourage* fame and his wife. On this particular night, though, he was far and away the B-lister, because two tables down from them, nestled in the corner, were Paul McCartney and his wife, Nancy Shevell.

As they passed the Dillon table on their way out, Kevin struck up a conversation with Sir Paul. The pleasantries were fairly routine, certainly nothing exceptional enough to warrant the lack of brevity customary for a nothing-special-on-your-way-out-the-door chat. You could clearly tell that Shevell, who was standing behind her husband, seemingly eager to leave, had been in this situation many times. That's the price that comes with being married to an ex-Beatle: everyone wants a little conversational piece of him. She graciously apologized to us for slightly crowding our table, with a facial expression that implied, "I'm sure you can appreciate that this happens fairly often." She patiently stood by while the exchange lasted a polite length of time, after which she raised her hand to rub the middle of her husband's back, in what is the universal spousal signal for "Okay, honey, let's wrap this up and get going."

OVERSTAYING YOUR WELCOME

In almost every encounter we have, there is a sweet spot for how much of someone else's time we should take up. Too brief and you can appear disinterested, abrupt, and curt. Too long and you run the risk of being labeled "one of those people," the big bag of wind others can't seem to get away from fast enough. I live in constant fear of the latter. In fact, I have a recurring nightmare that I am in front of a packed audience about halfway through my rehearsed talk, when the digital countdown clock in front of me hits zero. But there I am, still yakking away. From somewhere over the foot of the stage, I hear an orchestra play the music from the Oscars that signals, "No more talking . . . take your award and get off stage NOW!" That very real fear has done more to help keep me concise than almost anything else.

IS SPEAKING CONCISELY A CHALLENGE FOR YOU?

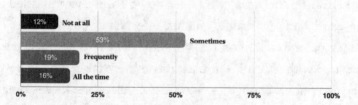

My own allergic reaction to overstaying my conversational welcome has made me more acutely aware of others struggling to find the right balance. When we asked people in our survey how often they struggle with being concise, more people said "frequently" or "all the time" than the number that claimed "not at all." The number of people who responded "sometimes" was more than double any other answer.

When I begin working with a new client, I always ask the same question: "If you could be self-analytical for a moment, what aspect of your communication capabilities would you most like to improve?" Inevitably, the area of concern that I hear most often is brevity. Most people say they have less difficulty getting started than they do wrapping it up. The problem is more than just blowing through the conversational stop signs. It's about not even knowing where the stop signs are. This can often be the result of speaking without a clear sense of purpose as to what idea you're trying to communicate, or the scourge of talking just to hear yourself talk in the hopes that miraculously the point you're trying to make will magically appear during a ceaseless yammer. I call this the Michael Scott Syndrome, an homage to Steve Carell's character in *The Office*. In a scene from that show, Scott admits in a moment of extreme candor, "Sometimes I start a sentence, and I don't even know where it's going. I just hope I find it along the way . . . like an improv conversation, an improversation."

MORE IS NOT MORE

If you dig down into the deepest recesses of your mind, back to a time before there was GPS, you know that if you had a fuzzy idea of how to drive to your destination, it not only took you longer to get there, but the lack of certainty made you drive more tentatively. The same holds true for how we speak. Frequently we get lost in our own sea of words, adrift in a meandering, disjointed stream of consciousness. For all that's been written about the importance of being concise, we humans still struggle mightily with the concept. For some misguided reason, we think more is more, that we can be much more eloquent speaking for a full minute than ten seconds. Even worse, when others challenge us and criticize our point of view, we tend to talk even more, mistakenly thinking that the longer we speak, the more convincing we'll be. Research draws a link between being challenged and the anxiety that can lead to over-talking. Joseph Burgo, psychologist and author of *Why Do I Do That?*, asserts that defensive reactions are the result of a person feeling, among other things, criticized and attacked. That in turn has ripple effects in communication: "Overtalking often arises from **social anxiety**, which creates a troubling feedback loop. The more people talk, the more anxious they become about their social selves, and the more they talk."

Our survey found that four potential causes for overtalking were somewhat equally to blame for people's lack of brevity: public-speaking nerves, lack of thorough preparation, getting into the weeds, and fear that if one little item is omitted from a presentation, they'll appear not to have been thorough.

WHAT PREVENTS YOU FROM SPEAKING MORE CONCISELY?

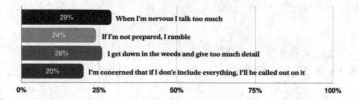

In my experience, brevity frequently has a direct correlation to the knowledge and preparedness of the presenter. I can often tell which sections of a presentation people feel the least confident about by the amount of time they take to explain them. When a presenter has great command of the information, their clarity of thought allows them to nail the point concisely and move on. Their knowledge of the subject matter also makes it more likely that they will be able to break down their point of view to simple concepts, as Albert Einstein once observed: "If you can't explain it simply enough, you don't understand it well enough."

At the risk of sounding like I'm trying to improve on Einstein (a fool's errand if ever there was one), I would also stipulate that, if you don't understand it well enough, you can't explain it concisely enough.

X USED TO MARK THE SPOT

As a lifelong proponent of brevity, I enthusiastically applauded Twitter's mandate when they first launched in 2006 that tweets had to be kept to 140 characters or less. Eliminating that requirement eleven years later was, in my opinion, one of the worst policy decisions in social media history. When people need less space to communicate their ideas, they are forced to be pithier, punchier, and ultimately more memorable. That character limit was one of the few effective motivators to get us to stop talking so damn much. That's why I've often fantasized about inventing a device that could put an end to ceaseless yammering once and for all. Just as a pedometer or smart watch measures the number of steps you take each day, I want to create a simple piece of technology that counts the number of words we speak in any given day. With the possible exception of cloistered monks, the average person utters 16,000 words a day. That seems like a staggering amount, doesn't it? What percentage of those do you think are absolutely necessary? I would be shocked if even three-quarters of them are essential for communicating what needs to be said.

SHEDDING UNWANTED PARAGRAPHS

How did I come up with that estimated percentage? Because after I write an email, I look it over and ask myself, what can I easily get rid of here? What wording is nonessential to the overall message? On average, 25 percent of it gets deleted on the first pass of editing. That's a quarter of the content eliminated from the most cursory effort, a totally achievable milestone. That's why to our most loquacious clients, I propose that we put them on a "verbal diet." Instead of 16,000 words a day, I suggest they limit themselves to 12,000. While that may seem like an aggressive dose of verbal Ozempic, it is precisely the right threshold to inspire people to be more targeted and more selective when they speak. If you knew that you had four thousand fewer words to play with every day, imagine how much more efficient and thoughtful you would be in communicating. The consequence of being long-winded would be using up your allotment of words by four o'clock in the afternoon and not being allowed to say anything until midnight, when your supply automatically replenished. Blowing your verbal budget before the end of the day would force you to communicate with your work colleagues as if you were playing a game of charades.

The key to sticking to your leaner word count is planning and preparation. When you approach any communication opportunity, having a crystal-clear notion of how the narrative is going to roll off your tongue allows you to be more concise and more efficient in getting to the point. Confidence based on your belief that nobody knows more about this subject than you do, and that therefore you can "wing this," is one of the biggest pitfalls I see in communication. Misguided confidence, or overconfidence, is merely an invitation to ramble. Think of it like packing for a trip. If you're a good strategic packer, you probably carefully select exactly what you're going to need, and you lay the clothes out on your bed in advance. This is akin to the content creation. Now, the actual act of packing, of putting the clothes in the suitcase, is quick and easy, as would be the delivery of your message. But if you're a chaotic packer, one who rummages through your drawers and closet pulling out every single possibility, three things occur: the packing takes longer, you often overpack, and frequently you discover in the midst of the trip that you didn't even bring the right clothes. All of this results from poor planning and preparation.

When you exercise portion control in the thoughts you share, you crystallize your message by eliminating extraneous, meaningless, and distracting content. The other benefit to being kept on a tight word count is the decreased likelihood that you will make a critical mistake or say something you regret. I also liken communicating to skiing. When you first start out, your energy keeps you upright and in control. But the more you continue, a certain fatigue factor kicks in and accidents become more likely. Ask any skier and they'll probably tell you that it's usually on that last run of the day, when your legs are a bit tired, that you are more prone to falling and breaking a leg. In my experience, people are at greater risk of saying something damaging forty-five or sixty seconds into a thought than they are in the first twenty. Don't underestimate the role fatigue plays in communication. Why do you think experienced and shrewd journalists do everything they can to keep their interview subjects talking? Because they know that inevitable verbal fatigue could very well prompt a slipup that generates a juicy, clickbait headline.

EMPTY-CALORIE WORDS

Since we're striving to get more verbally fit, how about we rid ourselves of the dreaded empty calories that add unwanted bloat to our communications? I'm talking about filler words. "Um, so, like, uh, kind of, sort of" are the trans fat–laden bag of chips in our communication cupboard. They are the Cheetos of chatter. They don't add anything nutritionally valuable to what we have to say, and perhaps more than any other verbal tendency, they erode our perceived executive presence. If you are intent on advancing in your career, and being seen as a potential leader, my advice is to aggressively work to eliminate the filler. I have had high-ranking corporate executives ask me to work on the presentation skills of one of their colleagues with a dire ultimatum: "This person's communication skills must improve or there is no future growth potential for them at this company." At the time I remember thinking that it was an ominously stark and harsh assessment of this person's future. But as time has passed, I have come to understand the reasoning. How we communicate is our calling card, the barometer for how others gauge our gravitas. Filler language is like putting childlike scribbling all over that calling card.

KICKING THE JUNK-WORD HABIT

I'm not going to pretend that eradicating filler words is easy. In fact, it may very well be one of the most difficult communication tasks you've ever attempted. By accepting this challenge, you are aiming to reverse speaking habits that have become deeply ingrained over time. If you've wondered why kicking the filler-word habit is so difficult, there's a special reason why it can be especially hard. Russell Poldrack of Stanford University did research on the topic. "Changing behavior in lasting ways is really difficult. Individuals tend to revert to their first-learned behavior during times of stress or when they experience difficulty sustaining the attention needed to persist with their newly adopted behaviors." Both of those situations occur when you're presenting: it's stressful and most of us are devoting all of our attention to the task at hand, with nothing left over to concentrate on not saying the filler words.

Regardless of how favorable or unfavorable the odds are of kicking the filler-language habit, consider it a professional imperative if you don't want flawed communication skills to hold you back. As in most behavioral-changing campaigns, I want you to embrace a simple three-step program.

Step 1—Awareness: I would wager that you are unaware of how often you use filler words, and even possibly which ones you are most prone to using. So, let's find out. Next time you have to give a work presentation or lead a meeting, take out your phone and record yourself. Apps like Otter AI will not only record audio, but they will provide a transcript as well. Recording for about ten minutes should provide you with a substantial sampling. Comb through the transcript and see which filler words you favor and how frequently you use them. If you want to take Operation Filler Kill to the next level, you could invest in software like Yoodli, that will record any virtual meeting, provide a transcript, *and* tally up for you all the filler words you say. It's a fabulous, if not sobering, tool. The goal is to get your filler words to less than 3 percent of the total word count.

Recently I trained an intelligent and promising young executive who had been promoted to the C-suite, a career advancement she was eager to prove was well deserved. Over the course of a two-hour coaching session, she said "you know" 344 times. "Like," which is often used instead of "said," was uttered 295 times, and "um" 234 times. A big contributor to this was her pace. A desirable speaking speed is around 150 words per minute. She was clocked at 234! The good news is, when you temper your verbal thirst for speed, the filler language abates. So, once you identify your brand of filler, you're ready to move on.

Step 2—Slow down! For most of us, filler language is a product of speaking too quickly. The faster we go, the more susceptible we are to falling into that trap. Think of a filler word as that big pothole in the road we mentioned earlier. It's just a couple of hundred feet in front of you. If you're driving fast, you have less time to react and steer around it. Filler words are always lurking just around every conversational corner. Since our brains, on average, are only about 600 milliseconds ahead of our mouths, there's very little time to vet or filter the words your brain has chosen for your mouth to articulate. But if you lengthen the pipeline connecting the brain and the mouth, by even a few extra milliseconds, you can better detect that filler word that's coming up. Admittedly, it's hurtling through that pipeline at breakneck speed, but like that pothole, it is possible to see it in advance and consciously discard it before you say it. The truth is, merely slowing your pace might not be enough to rid yourself of the dreaded filler. Creating a longer brain–mouth pipeline may require leveraging one of the most powerful yet underutilized tools available to all communicators.

Step 3—The power of the pause: A well-known quote from Mozart, "The music is not in the notes, but in the silence in between," could apply just as well to public speaking. There are many important benefits to pausing. It can help bold and underline your big ideas, it can give you more opportunities to breathe in the middle of sentences (so you're not gasping for air in between sentences), and perhaps most importantly, it can dramatically reduce the filler words that infiltrate our speech. Sometimes the best way to avoid that pothole is to come to a full and complete stop before you get to it.

MINDLESS MUMBLING

Another similarity between filler words and the empty calories of junk food is the role stress plays in both. For many people, the more anxiety they're experiencing, the more likely they are to reach for something they know they shouldn't be eating. That's because the hormone cortisol increases in the body when we're under stress. High cortisol levels can increase our cravings for sugary or fatty foods, which is why I'm sure the snack food companies have zero interest in seeing our collective stress levels go down. Not surprisingly, there is data to suggest a correlation between economic downturns and global disasters and increased snack food sales. When we communicate under stress, not only are we less capable of modifying our behavior, but our speaking pace can change because of the body's release of adrenaline. When we're stressed, communication becomes faster and more impulsive, and the amount of careful consideration of our word choices declines. The less selective we are, the less we are able to implement steps two and three of our plan.

THE GMO OF WORDS

Just as eating whole, nutritious foods is a cornerstone of a healthy diet, using real, legitimate words is another aspect of a healthy verbal diet. Any nutritionist will tell you that ingredients on the label you can't pronounce are bad for you. Yet that's what overtook the food industry in the 1950s. Processed foods that contained a lot of chemicals and additives to increase the convenience and shelf life of products proliferated in supermarkets. When a jar of mayonnaise takes more than three years to go bad in your refrigerator, you know that what's inside is more artificial than real. The communication equivalent of processed food is jargony language, words that if you wrote them on your computer, a red line would appear underneath them, words like "moderninity." My ironclad rule of thumb? If there's a red line underneath that word, it shouldn't be coming out of your mouth. Like artificial ingredients in processed food, jargon can make us conversationally bloated.

Recently a client was telling me how much she struggled with jargon and that she needed to "decomplexify" her communication. At first I thought she was putting me on. But she said it with a completely straight face. "Wouldn't the word 'simplify' be better there? The dictionary is chock-full of lots of good words," I suggested. "I think we can make do with what's already in there." Jargon is insidiously pervasive and corrosive to our ability to communicate clearly and effectively. Ironically, people employ jargon to sound intelligent, but it only has the opposite effect. It makes them sound like an empty suit. I could write a whole book on the scourge of jargon, but instead I've decided to follow my own advice and truncate it all into Chapter 6 of this book.

Another bizarre communication trend is using nouns as verbs. I see and hear it all around me. On the subway, a hotel chain is imploring me through one of their print ads to "guest the way you guest." I'm willing to grant double-duty status to "vacation," which works as both a noun and a verb. Maybe even "holiday" (although that's somewhat of a stretch), but "guest"? Knowing how Madison Avenue thinks, perhaps they are hoping that seeing a word grossly misused will make you focus on the message for just a split second longer. But my heart goes out to the poor, beleaguered noun, that overworked and underpaid part of speech. While all its grammatical peers are kicking back and relaxing, the noun is constantly asked to carry more and more of the conversational load. If grammatical parts of speech were coworkers at a company, you could almost imagine the verb laughing under its breath, as it sees the noun getting called into Human Resources to have its workload dramatically increased. The scene might go something like this:

HR DIRECTOR: Good morning, Noun. I'm Peter Palaver. From a scheduling perspective, it's a solid value-add that you were able to restack your myriad of calendar commitments in such an expeditious way so that we could have some constructive face-time.

NOUN: You mean you're glad I could swing by on such short notice? Of course. I got your email first thing this morning saying it was important. Is everything okay?

HR DIRECTOR: From an employment standpoint, everything remains status quo given the current staffing structural ecosystem.

NOUN: So you're not firing me? Oh good. I was a little nervous on the way over here. But I tried to remind myself how important I am to our communication. I mean, it would be pretty hard to form a sentence without me.

HR DIRECTOR: The integral nature of your contributions is indisputable. Rather from an org-chart perspective, I want to engage you with both authenticity and intentionality in a dialogue I have been supremely choiceful about: namely your core competencies and regions of responsibility.

NOUN: So you're changing my job description?

HR DIRECTOR: We're commencing with a downsizing and a reorging simultaneously so we will be requiring a finite group of thought leaders to partake in upskilling exercises and assume some incremental challenges. From time immemorial, management has had you covering three verticals: persons, places, and things.

NOUN: Yeah. It sure does keep me busy. Being a part of every subject and just about every object has had me pulling double duty ever since I can remember.

HR DIRECTOR: Yes, we have been thorough in leveraging and amortizing your talents in that manner, Noun. But the ELT has ideated on this matter and in our quest to bring innovation to our lexicon and reimagine from first principles how we bring flawless execution to our articulation, we're going to ask you to assume a fourth vertical in conjunction with your current responsibilities. We believe this will have impact all along the value chain.

NOUN: So the bosses want me to do more? Who's not pulling their weight? Adverbs? I agree you could do away with them and every sentence would be better off.

HR DIRECTOR: No. Basically, we wholeheartedly believe adverbs are essentially a key component to our ongoing campaign to fully and uniquely hyperbolize our communication efforts. No, Noun, we need you to be a verb now too.

NOUN: I don't understand.

HR DIRECTOR: We're doubling down on our need to bring more action to each and every sentence.

NOUN: But asking me to be a verb as well would be like asking an exclamation point to also be a question mark. Perhaps you can explain how you see this working.

HR DIRECTOR: Here on this Excel spreadsheet I've outlined a number of suggestions. For instance, currently you're responsible for the word "effort." Now you would also assume the word "efforting." Instead of saying we're "doing our due diligence on this project," we are suggesting merely "we have diligenced this project." That's a savings of two whole words.

NOUN: All right, well, I guess I'll do my best. But can we meet again, say in six months to see how it's going? Is that what you call tabling the discussion?

HR DIRECTOR: Excellent, Noun! See, you're already acclimating nicely to this new way of thinking. Yes, an assessment review in six months. Let's calendar that.

THE LEXICON CLEANSE

If you're already a devotee of clean labels for the food you buy, extending that mindset to a clean vocabulary might be easier than you think. The trick is *not* to emulate your work colleagues' communication style, since theirs is likely riddled with jargon. What may be necessary is a lexicon cleanse, four weeks of disciplined communication in which you refuse to succumb to all jargon. Speaking in plain, simple language will make you a nonconformist, and when it comes to distinguishing yourself as a communicator, that's a good thing. I've had clients confidentially admit that refraining from jargon makes them feel a bit like an outsider and that they don't quite have the same sense of belonging they once had. Embrace that! That's a club in which you don't want membership. When I see a corporate executive communicate free of jargon, I immediately attribute greater leadership qualities to them. When they demonstrate the ability to be inspirational and motivational in clean, simple language, it reminds me how impressed I am with a comedian who succeeds in being funny without the need to constantly use vulgarity as a crutch.

Getting out of your comfort zone is always good guidance, but it's particularly valuable here. Remember our prime directive in communication: BE MEMORABLE! If you are leaning on the same overused, empty-calorie expressions as everyone else, it makes it nearly impossible to stand out and leave a memorable impression on your audience.

Above all, taking a long, circuitous route to making your point is an invitation to lose people. And yet, somewhere rummaging around in the backs of our brains is this fallacy that the longer I talk, the more convincing I'm going to be. But after a while, going on and on starts to compromise the appearance of conviction in your own thoughts, as if you're trying to convince yourself of the validity of your idea.

There's a handful of reasons why many of us can't resist saddling up to the all-you-can-say buffet, where "that idea looks good, let me help myself to a little of that," and "I can't not pile those granular details atop my already overflowing plate." My best advice? Selectively order à la carte off the menu and leave your captivated audience delightfully satiated instead of unnecessarily bloated.

SAY THIS	NOT THAT
"specialties"	"bespoke specialisms"
"treating our pets like family"	"humanization of domesticated animals"
"They work well together"	"They achieve complementarity"
"where we come into contact with it"	"across all the various touchpoints"

PART III

STICKY TALK

If your top public-speaking goals are to stand out from the crowd and be remembered, these next three chapters are for you. You're about to embark on a guided tour through a multitude of tips, tricks, and techniques that can transform even the most routine and mundane business presentation into a captivating narrative that rattles around in your audience's noggin for a few days, a few weeks, or even longer. The more memorable you are, the more impact you will have.

4

THE THEORY OF LEVITIVITY

"Harold...I said start your speech with some levity, not levitation."

It was a crisp October morning in New York City and a throng of wealthy investors (or as they're labeled in the investment world, "high-net-worth individuals") were flocking to the Plaza hotel to determine whether the hedge fund in which they had invested was properly meeting their expectations for more wealth generation. Such is the reason why nearly every investment firm holds an annual conference called "Investor Day." At these events, typically the heads of various divisions give a presentation outlining past performance, what drove that performance, and where the economy is likely headed. If you had no skin in the game, the contents would strain your ability to stay awake. On this particular morning, however, a group of serious investors saw something in one of the presentations that I guarantee none of them ever expected to see: a clip from the screwball comedy classic movie *The Naked Gun*. Yes, you heard me correctly, *The Naked Gun*. Talk about an investment conference crasher! It sounds like an unlikely stretch, but it was a stroke of imaginative genius that worked perfectly because it was so unexpected. That's what made it memorable.

SETTING UP THE ZANY GAG

The narrative to be conveyed was that the U.S. economy seemed to be in an unstoppable period. All the typical roadblocks to economic growth were not slowing it down: uncertainty with emerging markets, threats of trade wars, and the United Kingdom's "Brexit" from the European Union. And like anything that has had the brakes fail, the only way to stop it seemed to be a "hard landing" or a crash. Placed in unimaginative hands, the communication of these points could be a real snoozer. But the senior managing director, an executive I worked with for many years, was a real devotee of injecting some imaginative fun into dry topics, which in my book is one of the greatest public-speaking talents you can possess. Kudos to him for seeing the metaphorical connection between those economic factors and a scene in *The Naked Gun* in which Leslie Nielsen's character, police lieutenant Frank Drebin, is in a car chase with a bad guy whose vehicle is supposed to represent the runaway U.S. economy. While trying to get away, the bad guy's car inadvertently slams into a gasoline tanker truck. Even though the collision ignites a fiery explosion, it doesn't slow down his momentum. The clip is briefly paused to identify the gas truck as a symbol of the threat of future trade wars. From there, it gets more hysterically preposterous. The bad guy's getaway car then smashes into an army tank carrying a missile, which is meant to symbolize Brexit. The ensuing fireball is even more dramatic, yet the escape vehicle only seems to gain steam. Ultimately the bad guy's flight comes to a full stop when he slams into a fireworks factory. The massive pyrotechnics that result are likened to a recent stock market plunge, which did indeed have a chilling effect on the U.S. economy. The final analogous connection made was by comparing Drebin, who tells onlookers gawking at the mile-high explosions, "disperse . . . nothing to see here," to the chairman of the Federal Reserve, Jerome Powell, who many believed was seriously downplaying the market collapse.

When the managing director told me his idea to play this clip in his presentation, I could see the concern on his face, that he thought I'd tell him he was nuts. It's very possible that others he had run the idea past had questioned his sanity. After all, the conventional wisdom says that you should always play to your audience, and this one tended to be a well-heeled, old-money crowd.

Most people think that the more serious the venue and the more buttoned-up the subject matter, the less opportunity there is to inject levity. There was always the possibility that to this investor audience, a naked gun means a pistol not in its holster. So, when he put the question directly to me, "Do you think I should use this?" I replied with a swift and enthusiastic "Hell yeah!"

"Really? You really think so?" he said, seeking ironclad reassurance.

"My insistence," I told him, "is based on one universal truth. Everyone, no matter what audience they're a part of, enjoys a laugh." That truism was resoundingly supported in our Clarity Media Group survey, when we asked respondents whether they like a presenter who uses humor. Ninety-seven percent said yes.

DO YOU ENJOY WORK PRESENTATIONS THAT INCORPORATE HUMOR?

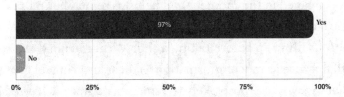

At Investor Day, my client played the clip in his presentation, and to our delight (and relief) the audience howled with laughter. In fact, our survey also showed that roughly the same percentage viewed the presenter more favorably, whether that was remembering what they said, seeing them as more confident, or liking them better. You don't have to be a hedge fund manager to know that's good ROI (return on investment).

This humorously-ever-after tale does not bely the stark reality that the use of levity is the ultimate high-wire act of public speaking, the epitome of high risk, high reward. The exhilaration of making an audience laugh is hard to match. Many accomplished communicators say that getting a laugh early in a speech or presentation helps calm nerves and boost confidence. Beyond that, humor also helps you display empathy and showcases intelligence in a way that doesn't come across as arrogant.

These were the findings of a study at the Stanford University Graduate School of Business by behavioral scientist and professor Jennifer Aaker and lecturer Naomi Bagdonas: "Humor does more than just make people laugh. It allows you to connect with your audience, diffuse tension, elevate status, foster trust, and compel others to your point of view. Humor can also help you and your message stand out, yet most of us hesitate to use humor, especially in our professional lives."

In my efforts to encourage clients to add humor, I find their attitude toward levity is not unlike how they might think about setting off fireworks: fun, exciting, spectacular, but oh so dangerous if you're a novice who doesn't know what you're doing. But the best argument I make when trying to convince them to take the comedic plunge is the stickiness factor. The Stanford research showed that humor makes us more engaged in the moment and helps us remember more content after the fact. In one study, researchers found that people who watched a humorous film clip before taking a short-term memory test recalled more than twice as much information as those in a control group. Perhaps that's why we're more likely to remember a story delivered by Jon Stewart or Stephen Colbert than by Anderson Cooper.

A study from the Annenberg School for Communication at the University of Pennsylvania and the School of Communication at Ohio State University supports the idea that in public speaking you have a choice: be funny, or be forgettable. The research found that humor was a key contributor to both virality and retention. A group of young adults (eighteen to thirty-four years old) were shown news stories about politics and government policy that were both humorous and nonhumorous. The study concluded that the viewers were not only more likely to share the humorous ones with others online, but they were also more likely to remember the content from these segments. Yet, in my experience coaching public speakers, presentations are often pretty humorless affairs.

REASONS BEHIND THE RELUCTANCE

One of the biggest reasons you don't see more levity in public speaking is that people have been burned by bad counsel. For years, presenters have been told, "Start off with a joke, they'll love it!" That is the single worst piece of advice you can get, even worse than "picture the audience in their underwear." If anyone ever recommends either of these strategies to you, run as fast as you can in the opposite direction. Leave the formal joke-telling to professional comedians. Instead, think of your job as finding a humorous lens through which you want the audience to view your content. For example, in my coaching sessions, when I urge people not to read their slides verbatim, I refer to that bad habit as "slide karaoke." While not a sidesplitter, it never fails to bring a smile to people's faces.

In our Clarity Media Group survey, other factors came to light that help explain why humor can be scant in professional settings. While 45 percent of people said they always try to find a way to include humor, 54 percent indicated they leaned against it, either because they didn't know how to do it, were afraid the attempt could bomb and it would backfire, or feared it would make them seem unprofessional.

WHAT'S YOUR OPINION OF USING HUMOR IN SPEECHES OR PRESENTATIONS?

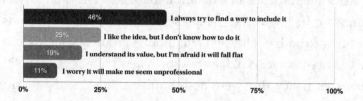

IT'S NO JOKE

The biggest shift in mindset that helps people be successful with humor is understanding the difference between telling a joke and injecting levity and humor into your content. The two are very different. In the presentations I've given over the years, I have never told a joke in the way a professional comedian does. That skill is way above my pay grade. But this conflation is at the heart of the problem in the corporate world.

Over the years, I've encountered more than my share of corporate communications people who have asked me to break the news to one of their execs that they're no Dave Chappelle, and that perhaps starting meetings and presentations with a traditional joke is a tactic ready for retirement. Frankly, I'd rather tell them their wardrobe stinks. At least you can fix that with one decent shopping spree. Last time I checked, the joke-telling gene cannot be medically added to our strands of DNA, at least not yet. The suggestion to refrain gets even tougher when the exec thinks that always opening with a joke is part of their trademark.

But while natural comedic talent isn't something that everyone's born with, you can learn to effectively incorporate humor into speeches and presentations. Utilized correctly, it can be one of the most powerful tools in your public-speaking toolkit to captivate an audience.

HOW THE PROS DO IT

To help you on this course, which for some of you might be uncharted territory, I sought out the advice of one of the very few people who have written comedy at both the highest levels of late-night television and the pinnacle of the corporate world. Nell Scovell was the only woman in the writer's room of *Late Night with David Letterman* and the chief speechwriter for former Meta COO Sheryl Sandberg, as well as many other titans of industry.

"When you say something funny," Nell said, "it usually implies a cultural reference that everyone shares. And so, when everyone laughs at it, it makes them feel like they're a community."

Scovell believes the target we should all shoot for is the area between getting outside your comfort zone and staying within your skill level for being funny. The trick, she says, is to not overreach.

"I think for a longer joke, you need some chops and you need some sense of comedic rhythm. But I think anyone can make a funny observation and get a laugh. You just want to lower the degree of difficulty for yourself." Her advice to those for whom humor doesn't come easily is, "You don't have to make the whole Thanksgiving dinner. You could just make a couple of side dishes." And just like the cooking axiom that you should never cook a dish for company that you've never made before, even if it's merely a side dish, you should never attempt humor in public speaking that hasn't been road-tested on someone whose opinion you respect.

"I do think it's always good to start with something clever, something positive, something upbeat, whether that's a joke or not," she said. "I will say comedy is hard because it's not guaranteed."

That lack of guarantee could be a contributing factor as to why less than half of respondents in our poll said that they

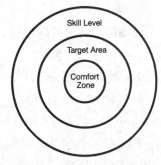

---

used humor in presentations either all the time or frequently. But at the same time, 95 percent acknowledged the benefits it brings, such as seeing the speaker as more likeable, more confident, or more memorable.

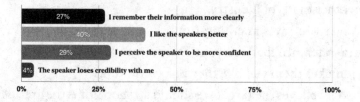

HOW DO YOU REACT WHEN OTHERS USE HUMOR IN PRESENTATIONS?

Scovell crafted a speech Sheryl Sandberg gave at the University of California, Berkeley that started off not with a joke, but with a funny line that was part of what sounded like merely the obligatory opening thank-yous:

"It is a privilege to be here at Berkeley, which has produced so many Nobel Prize winners, Turing Award winners, astronauts, members of Congress, Olympic gold medalists . . . and *that's just the women.*"

The element of humor deployed in that open is a surprise, in which a mundane setup is followed by an unexpected conclusion.

THE SCIENCE BACKS IT UP

The science tells us that the rewards for adding humor far outweigh the risks that come with no guarantees. The researchers who carried out the University of Pennsylvania study also collected data on the participants' brain activity using fMRI technology. What they found was that humorous news clips elicited greater activity in brain regions associated with thinking about what other people think and feel, which high-lights the critical role of empathy, which we will discuss in Chapter 9.

The human biology that explains why humor helps you have more impact when you speak involves dopamine, the hormone in our bod-ies that Harvard Health called "the pathway to pleasure." Dopamine gets released in our bodies in conjunction with a lot of activities that rank right up there on most people's greatest-hits list: smelling cook-ies baking in the oven, shopping, sex, and, of course, hearing some-thing funny. When dopamine hits our brains, it generates pleasure and makes us feel good.

This chain reaction can be particularly welcome in the confines of the workplace, which sometimes—let's face it—can lack a little pizzazz. But humor has the capacity to deliver a counterintuitive, two-pronged benefit. In addition to flooding the brain with pleasure, it also can help lift us out of the stress pit that our offices often can be, by delivering a calming effect. And when things are a bit tense around the office, who wouldn't like to have a little more of that?

COMIC RELIEF = PAIN RELIEF

Laughter's role as a stress-buster is supported by studies at the Mayo Clinic: they found that laughter can "activate and relieve your stress response." It does this by increasing the endorphins that are released by your brain. Laughter, they concluded, soothes tension by stimulating circulation and aiding in muscle relaxation, both of which can help re-duce some of the physical symptoms of stress. But it goes beyond that. If you've ever watched your favorite comedian do a stand-up routine and noticed that an ache or pain you're dealing with subsided a bit, it's not your imagination. The Mayo Clinic's study also found laughter may actually ease pain by causing the body to produce its own natural painkillers.

Another benefit not to be underestimated is laughter's impact on our confidence. Bringing laughter to others was found to boost self-esteem, a critical factor in projecting executive presence during speeches and presentations. Not coincidentally, when people in our survey were asked what skills they would most like to acquire to enhance their public speaking, overwhelmingly the top two responses were confidence and humor.

EVERYBODY JUST RELAX!

Sometimes, when speaking in front of a group of people, we get so caught up in our own battle with nerves that we lose sight of the fact that the reverse is also true. The audience is experiencing their own nervousness. As intimidating as the faces of your audience may look from your position at the front of the room or onstage, the audience is rooting for you to do well. That little evil voice on your shoulder that's trying to convince you that the audience is just waiting for you to mess up royally is pouring unproven poison in your ear that can strip you of your confidence and undermine your performance. Humor, especially right at the beginning, can help release that audience tension and put them in a better state to receive what you have to say. It bears repeating, though, don't start with a random joke. If it bombs, it could take a few precious moments to recover from it, if you recover at all. Instead, tell a real story that has humorous elements to it. One of my favorite examples is a TED Talk that educator and social activist Geoffrey Canada gave a few years ago. Canada, a champion for improving education for underserved communities, began by giving the audience access to a private conversation he had had with his wife the day before, something audiences always love: being a fly on the wall overhearing something that maybe they weren't supposed to:

> I'm a little nervous because my wife, Yvonne, said to me, she said, "Geoff, you watch the TED Talks?"

I said, "Yes, honey. I love TED Talks."

She said, "You know they're like really smart, talented . . ."

I said, "I know, I know."

This opening brilliantly navigates the delicate balance of self-deprecation. A little bit goes a long way. Too much and you risk undermining yourself. Here Canada humorously endears himself to the audience by admitting that his wife is wiser than he is, a technique Barack Obama used at the 2024 Democratic National Convention when he came out immediately after Michelle Obama gave her rousing speech and opened by saying, "I am the only person stupid enough to speak after Michelle Obama."

Canada's story continued with a warning from his wife: "They don't want like . . . the angry Black man."

The audience erupted with laughter.

"No, I'm gonna be good, honey, I'm gonna be good. But I *am* angry." The audience erupts again, and after a perfect pause for comedic timing, he looks down at the color of the skin on his hand. "And the last time I looked . . ." Laughter now is mixed with applause for what the audience realizes is a well-constructed, funny open. They are now fully engaged and relaxed, eager to hear what Canada has come to share. Now the challenging part. How can he radically shift gears from something so lighthearted and funny to the seriousness of inequality in education without wrecking the transmission?

For Scovell, this often seems to some like an insurmountable challenge: "The other issue I come up against when I'm trying to convince people to be funny in their speeches is the idea of the transition. And I think they feel like, how can I be funny and then be serious?"

Canada uses the theme of him being "angry" to link a seemingly disconnected open to the main body of his talk, and he accomplishes that with just one line he says over the applause:

"So, here's why I'm excited but I'm angry." As he says this, his vocal delivery is brisk and breezy and his body movements are frenetically animated. That all changes as he transitions to the all-important second part of his statement, the line that compels the audience to pay attention and care: "This year, there are going to be millions of our children that we're going to needlessly lose." To punctuate this, he dramatically slows down into an emphatic delivery and his body language changes to a solemn and deliberate march across the stage. It looks so natural and spontaneous, but it's a carefully finessed delivery that can only come from relentless practice.

CONCISE AND CLEVER

A grand joke worthy of famous comedians may be overkill in a business setting, where just a little light cleverness is more than sufficient to get the job done. A great example of this occurred at a *Fortune* conference moderated by the CEO of Ariel Investments, Mellody Hobson, who also happens to be married to film legend George Lucas, a detail that I share only because it provides essential context for her funny moment.

The topic turned to diversity, and even though Hobson had a serious point to make, in her mind there was still room for a quick jab of levity: "The other thing that bothers me, and I have to say this, it's not with anger or any kind of anxiety, it's just disappointment, is that we are working on this. And we don't work on anything else that matters in our companies. You either do or you do not, as my husband wrote for Yoda. There is no try. You do not work on getting better earnings. You do not work on having a product that's better. If it's not good enough, customers aren't going to buy it. But for some reason, we've all been allowed to get in this conversation of working on diversity."

The brief allusion to Yoda brought down the house and cut the tension in the room. That's another superpower of humor. Tempered properly and with sensitivity to the situation, it can make it easier to discuss sensitive topics, deliver negative news, or cope with difficult situations. That was also part of the findings of the Mayo Clinic study. Earlier in my career, I took full advantage of this benefit, although I have to admit, I was completely unaware of what I was doing.

CUSHIONING THE BLOW

When I was in my twenties, I was the broadcast producer for the news program *Nightwatch*, which was hosted by the yet-to-be-publicly-disgraced Charlie Rose. At the time, those of us on the show knew he was a total buffoon, or as I often referred to him, "the most well-read imbecile on TV." But it would be more than thirty years before current and former members of his production staff would come forward and accuse him of various forms of sexual harassment. The #MeToo tide of 2017 swept Rose away, never to be seen or heard from on network television again.

Back then, I had the unenviable task in the control room of trying to keep Charlie to stick to the allotted times for the interviews when we taped the show. If he ignored my directions and ran long, it meant that a team of producers later would have to find ways to shorten it in an edit room, a real burden because our show didn't have enough staff to do this on a regular basis. But Charlie didn't care. Regularly, he would conduct a ten-minute interview that was earmarked for an eight-minute segment. Going two minutes over may not sound like a lot, but in television that's not a simple trim—it's major surgery. I tried everything to get him to stop, from strong-arm tactics to begging. Nothing worked. Then, one day, I went into his office with a different approach in mind.

One of the sources of comic relief for our bedraggled and demoralized staff (our motto was "free the Nightwatch 50," referring to our scant staff of fifty) were the vocal impressions I did of both Charlie and the show's executive producer. Being the ever-shameless narcissist, Charlie loved hearing my impressions of him. So, when I walked into his office, I went into my shtick, replicating his slight North Carolina drawl: "Listen, Billy McGowan, I'm the kind of rare talent who can't be confined by something as mundane as a clock. When I tap into my inner journalistic genius and dazzle audiences with my erudite conversations with the most interesting people on the planet, it's as if time is standing still." Clearly not realizing the degree to which I was mocking him, Charlie met the impression with approving laughter. But then it was time to make my point. So I shifted into the voice of the executive producer, "Listen, McGowan. If you can't get that imbecile to understand that the difference between ten minutes and eight minutes is two whole minutes, then it's your ass that'll get kicked to the curb. There's only one person watching who wants to hear him drone on for two extra minutes, and that's his mother."

When Charlie's laughter subsided, I said in all seriousness, "Charlie . . . unless you want to see me pounding the pavement looking for a new job, please do me a favor? Stick to your time cues . . . PLEASE!" From that point on, the situation improved dramatically.

EMBRACING THE RISK

Nell and I were both in a meeting with Sheryl Sandberg at Facebook as she was preparing for a speech she was giving at the U.S. Naval Academy in Annapolis, Maryland, as part of the Forrestal Lecture Series, an event featuring leaders from across various industries. It was a prestigious invite to get, but also one that carried extra pressure, given that Sheryl was going to be the first woman ever to address the midshipmen. Part of the speech spoke to the need for open and honest communication, and Sheryl and Nell had an idea to tell the following funny story:

"Now if you watch children, you immediately notice how amazingly honest they are. I'll give you an example. My friend, Betsy, was pregnant and her five-year-old son was asking her where the baby was in her body. 'Mommy,' he said, 'are the baby's arms in your arms?' 'No,' his mother replied, 'the whole baby is in my tummy.' 'Are the baby's legs in your

legs?' he persisted. 'No, the whole baby is in my tummy,' his mother as-
sured him. 'Really,' the boy said, 'the whole baby is in your tummy? Are
you sure?' 'Yes,' his mother repeated, 'the whole baby is in my tummy.'
'Then Mommy,' the boy asked, 'what is growing in your butt?'"

The story was a big hit, a story made even funnier by Sheryl's im-
peccable comedic timing. I doubt anyone in the audience that evening
could have imagined the level of her ambivalence about including it in
the days leading up to the speech. She wasn't sure how it would land,
so she asked for opinions from the half-dozen people at the meeting.
Nearly everyone discouraged her from using it, except for myself and
Nell. I told her, "Are you kidding? You *have to* tell that story. It may very
well be the only laugh you get." And sure enough, it was. The midshipmen loved it, and I'm certain that when they talk about the need for hon-
esty and transparency in their day-to-day lives, they think back on that
memorable speech, partly because her point was delivered with humor.

Sheryl's uncertainty over telling it was completely understandable.
Everyone feels anxiety from the nature of the risk. But women feel it
even more and with good cause. Studies show that the myriad of biases
that women face while communicating in the workplace even extends
to attempts at humor.

SHE'S NOT FUNNY? ARE YOU SERIOUS?

According to a 2019 study by the American Psychological Association,
the benefits of humor in the workplace reward men more highly than
women. Men who employ humor in work presentations are perceived
as having "higher levels of status" (respect, prestige) and receive "higher
performance ratings and leadership and capability assessments" compared to those who do not include humor. But the opposite is true
when women inject humor into work presentations. They're perceived
as having "lower status, lower levels of performance," and seem "less
capable as leaders."

The study was conducted as two controlled experiments to examine the impact gender has on the perception of humor. One male actor and one female actor were commissioned to play the role of a store manager. In a recorded presentation, both shared quarterly earnings to two other actors playing regional "managers." Each actor presented two versions. The first was made with five humorous statements sprinkled throughout, one being a short self-deprecating joke: "So, last night, my husband (wife) gave me some good advice about this presentation. He (she) said, whatever you do don't try to be too charming, witty, or intellectual . . . just be yourself!" *Ba-dum-bum!* The other version was presented without the joke.

The videos were shown to three hundred employees, both male and female, from various industries. The conclusion? Men and women's use of humor is interpreted differently. "The woman's use of humor was scored as less functional and more disruptive than the man's use of humor" by both the men and women who watched.

In the second experiment, responses were compared between the presentations using humor and those not including humor. "When the male manager added humor to the presentation, he was given higher ratings of perceived status, job performance, and leadership capability compared to when he did not include any humor. However, the opposite occurred for the female manager. Adding humor led to lower ratings of perceived status, job performance, and leadership capability."

The woman was viewed as having "poor judgment in jokes" and having tried "to cover up her lack of real business acumen by making little jokes." In contrast, the humorous male presenter was seen as "witty and likes to use humor to not seem like a stern speaker."

By no means does this research mean that women need to play it straight all the time. Instead, people need to be made aware of this form of bias. Research shows that the more exposure there is to this bias, the less likely it is to occur. The study concluded, "Ultimately, this can help women be more uninhibited in their use of humor at work, and organizations will be more likely to enjoy the positive outcomes of humor."

STAYING IN THE BIT

Another female executive who is wickedly funny and uses it to her advantage in public speaking is Kate White, author and former editor in chief of *Cosmopolitan*. Kate is a master at injecting a funny story into speeches and presentations, which made working with her a total laugh fest.

"Humor makes all the difference in the world for me when I'm giving a speech," she said. "I've got some Irish blood, and I grew up in a family where humor was very important, and we constantly made each other laugh, so I feel more authentic as a speaker if I've got some funny stories and asides packed in there."

She was preparing to speak to a group of female media executives and wanted to underscore, with a bit of self-deprecation, the complexities of managing a demanding job while being a hands-on parent. This story did the trick:

"I married a TV news anchor, which meant that I spent my weeknight evenings alone. That was tricky after we had a baby because it meant that once I got home at five thirty from my job, I was on my own. My husband, Brad, always called each night after the baby went to bed to ask how our time together had gone. One night, when I was still feeling a little harried after trying to manage everything, I told him, 'Good, good. We ate dinner and then I gave him a walk in the stroller, and then after we came back, we played for a while and then I read him a couple of little books. And after that I gave Hudson a bath and put him to bed.' There was this long pause and then my husband said, 'But his name is Hunter.'"

Terrific punch line! But on Kate's behalf, I wanted to get greedy. "They're going to really laugh at the payoff," I said, "but what if we extend the laugh with a short follow-up. How about you wait until the laughter starts to fade and then say with a vocal tone and facial expression that conveys annoyance over her husband calling her out on the mistake, 'Ugh, I knew it began with an H,' and deliver it as almost a throwaway line that seems totally spontaneous." That technique, called "staying in the bit," is a staple of professional comedians who seize every opportunity to keep the laughter momentum going. This extra line also utilizes the power of the unexpected. Everyone was expecting Kate to act guilty and sheepish that she messed up her own son's name, but instead they saw her react in a surprising way: she was irked and shrugged off her mistake as no big deal. From that point on, Kate had the audience in her pocket and was able to focus solely on her speech, without the distraction of worrying how she was coming across.

"Humor in a speech helps relax me, especially if I build it in within the first one to two minutes. The audience thinks, 'Hey, she's funny and I'm not going to be bored,' so that means as a speaker I can stop worrying about whether I'm going to win them over. I've already started to."

A MULTIFACETED TOOL

Studies indicate that humor brings a variety of benefits, and not just when you're standing in front of an audience. It can work magic in the workplace, contributing to a healthy corporate culture. For instance:

- It can boost employees' performance.
- It can increase job satisfaction.
- It has the power to relax people, and reduce stress.
- It can improve social relations.
- It can generate a positive mood, and increase motivation.

A GOOD ACT TO FOLLOW

When we recommend to clients that they bring some levity to their public speaking, invariably they ask, "Who outside of professional comedians would you recommend I watch?" Unhesitatingly, our answer is Barack Obama. We're certainly not going out on any limbs there. Even professional comedians agree. Recently, I asked *The Late Show* host Stephen Colbert who he thought was the funniest politician out of all the ones he's interviewed. Without hesitation he said, "Obama! His timing is incredibly good." It's an observation shared by Obama's former press secretary Jay Carney, even if the former president was a reluctant comic. "Comedic timing was one of his huge strengths. Every year he would have to do the White House Correspondents Dinner"—an event at which the president is expected to tell jokes—"and every year he would complain about having to do it. And as time went on, he would grow to like the material, and I would be up there on the stage with him. Invariably, every time afterwards we'd be leaving and he'd turn to me and say, 'That went pretty well, didn't it?' And I would reply, 'Yes, sir, it did.'"

THE HALO EFFECT

Properly applied, levity in public speaking can create an enormous halo effect, making your audience see you as intelligent, confident, empathetic, and approachable. What it does for your content is equally valuable—it gives it lasting power, and makes it memorable. That was the overwhelming finding in our survey in which 91 percent of respondents said that humor makes presentations more captivating.

DOES HUMOR MAKE WORK PRESENTATIONS MORE MEMORABLE?

OVERCOMING BLANK-PAGE SYNDROME

I've told you the importance of incorporating levity into your public speaking. I've shown you a few excellent examples of it being done well. But inevitably, you will have that dreaded experience of trying to start a speech or presentation with humor and that blank computer screen will start taunting you as it remains blank for way too long. Perhaps you want to use humor to enhance your leadership skills. For humor to be effective, a study reported by the National Institutes of Health determined, several factors must be considered:

1. **Situational context:** Ask yourself, do the composition of the audience and the topic of discussion lend themselves to the use of humor that's appropriate for that crowd? In other words, if you're a man speaking before an audience of female executives, it's probably a terrible idea to tell a story that pokes fun at your wife. Actually, on second thought, it's a lousy idea regardless of who is in the audience.

2. **Intention and motivation:** Be clear about your motivations and objectives for using humor. If it's not clear to your audience that you're trying to be funny, they could become confused and think you're wasting their time.

3. **Judgment and decision:** Factor in the emotional safety of your audience and choose humor that isn't likely to be insensitive or offensive.

4. **Skillful delivery:** Make use of all verbal and nonverbal skills: pausing, voice intonation, eye movement, hand gestures, facial expressions, and overall body language. Think about legendary comedian Rodney Dangerfield. His material would not be as funny without all the physical tics that made him seem like he's trying to wriggle free and escape from his suit and tie: the craning of his neck, the tugging at his shirt collar, the mopping of his brow with a handkerchief. The trick is to make the humorous line look spontaneous. Humor that comes across too rehearsed can lose its bite.

UNDERSTANDING REACTIONS

Know when enough is enough. If the audience thinks that you don't know when to stop or that you're oblivious to the fact that it's not funny anymore, they might question your social skills and the caliber of your judgment.

The best advice is to latch on to real stories of humorous situations that occur in your day-to-day life, write them down, and begin developing an archive. Amass as many as you can, because different amusing stories work in different situations. A tailor-made fit between the topic and tone of your humor and the sensibilities of your audience is the ultimate recipe for success.

I acknowledge that for some of you, humor simply may not be an option. Above all, I don't want you to try to be somebody you're not. For those of you in that camp, a terrific substitute for funny is clever, and there are many ways to demonstrate streaks of cleverness. That's what we'll explore in the next chapter.

DO THIS	NOT THAT
Share Humorous Observations	Tell a Random Joke
Keep the Levity Super Concise	Go for More Thinking You're on a Roll
Document Real-Life Amusing Stories	Craft Something Funny Not Based in Reality
Tailor Humor to Audience's Sensibilities	Employ the Same Humor with Every Audience

5

THE MAGNIFICENT SEVEN

"He's been trained to roll over and play dead when the speech starts to get boring."

In 1967, psychologist Albert Mehrabian of the University of California, Los Angeles, conducted a study on how the emotions of the speaker get conveyed and how they impact the listener. I frequently share the results of his findings in training sessions and they often shock people. What is most mystifying is not the three forms of communication that determine impact:

- the words you say
- how you say it
- your body language when you're saying it

What people find astounding is the order of importance assigned to each:

- 55 percent was determined by a speaker's body language
- 38 percent was the result of the speaker's vocal delivery
- 7 percent was attributed to the speaker's content

For anyone who has ever labored to convey their personal feelings and attitudes in writing, finessing and wordsmithing in an effort to flirt with perfection, this study, if misinterpreted, has to be discouraging. If you constantly work to elevate your content from merely good to exceptional, that statistic may have you wondering, "What's the point?"

After hearing tens of thousands of presentations over the years, the 7 percent number did not come as a surprise to me. Often, when presenters share their emotions and attitudes, they do so with all the passion associated with reading a spreadsheet of numbers. When the nonverbal expression behind personal attitudes is devoid of vocal variation and facial expressiveness, it becomes more difficult for the listener to derive the true meaning behind the words.

For years, Mehrabian's findings were misinterpreted to mean that only 7 percent of what audiences *remember* is based on the speaker's content. That mistakenly led presenters (and communication coaches) to think that words don't matter. But fifty-two years after his initial study, Mehrabian set the record straight in a media interview, declaring that "words have tremendous impact, absolutely!" So, don't be fooled into thinking that any old content is good enough. Additionally, if the content is less predictable and just a tad more clever and creative, the impact of the words will be even greater. As a presenter, what you should strive for is a reaction from your audience that says, "Wow, I love the way that idea was framed." Simply put, originality is a key to memorability.

MEMORABILITY'S HOLY GRAIL

I can't think of any greater source of pride than having a member of an audience you spoke to years ago come up to you and say, "I'll never forget something you told us that day you spoke to us. It still resonates with me today." Memorable communication reverberates and makes it possible for our language to achieve a legacy. When our words endlessly echo, that is the holy grail of communication.

There are seven effective tools that can make your ideas ricochet in people's heads for hours, days, or even weeks after you've said them. Let's call them the Magnificent Seven:

- Analogy/Metaphor
- Creative Label
- Twisted Cliché
- Wordplay
- Data with Context
- Original Definitions
- Mathematical Equations

They are techniques that you can learn and deploy, so your point of view and ideas not just land, but stick.

ANALOGY

One of the most effective devices to help get your point across is a well-crafted analogy. The reason why it's such an efficient tool is that with only a few words, you're able to help your audience comprehend a complex or unfamiliar concept by comparing it to something that's common to all our experiences. It doesn't matter what industry you work in: analogies work. Stephanie Ruhle, host on MSNBC, sees analogies as an ideal tool for reaching a vast audience in which the level of understanding varies widely:

"To me, analogies are the best, best, best. Politics is foreign to me and an analogy helps me. But where I have my greatest success is explaining business because I used to be on a network talking business to businesspeople. Now I go on the *Today* show and I talk business to a universe of people that are like 'la, la, la, I don't understand business.' So I need to make it plain for them. And analogies is the way you do it. I take complicated business topics and I break them down."

Within this analogy category, there are three different varieties: petite, medium, and jumbo. In an ideal world, we would make use of all three types in the interest of mixing it up. The worst thing that can happen to us as public speakers is to fall into predictable patterns.

What's most important to remember is that variance is the key to engagement and retention.

PETITE

You may be most familiar with the petite variety, given that a popular TV show used the device for its title: *Orange Is the New Black*. After Donald Trump was found guilty of thirty-four felony counts in June 2024, a twist on that show title was almost too obvious a meme:

The petite analogy is the punchiest of them all, making it also the most memorable. The effort to get Americans out of their chairs more frequently and create increased movement throughout the day (close that Apple Watch red ring!) gave rise to "Sitting is the new smoking."

Expanding the petite analogy with two or three additional parallels can make it even stronger. Staying with the tobacco theme, Salesforce CEO Marc Benioff in 2018 went on TV to proclaim that "Facebook is the new cigarettes." But he didn't leave it there, adding additional components to drive the comparison home: "You know it's addictive. It's not good for you. There's people trying to get you to use it that even they don't understand what's going on. It's guilty of false advertising, and therefore, it should be regulated." It was a provocative point of view delivered through a compelling communication device. That's a dynamic combo!

To explain how crowded the tequila market has become, thanks to the likes of Kendall Jenner, the Rock (Dwayne Johnson), and Brian Cranston launching their own brands, a memorable way to convey that thought could be: "Tequila is the new fragrance. Every celebrity is coming out with one."

The gaming industry has been focused on positioning videogames as the most dynamic core of entertainment. Increasingly, what ripples from that core are influences in the TV, music, and film industries. A petite analogy to articulate that could be: "Gaming is the hub of the twenty-first-century entertainment wheel."

MEDIUM

The medium analogy is the most common and also involves a direct comparison. Over the years, clients across a wide array of industries have shown keen interest in workshopping some memorable ones together.

In the logistics industry, executives have been asked over and over to explain the supply-chain crisis, a topic so complex that it could make seasoned professionals' eyes roll back in their head. A way to understand it, however, can rest in a simple visual parallel:

"At the height of the supply-chain woes, what we had was a six-lane

freeway trying to merge into a one-lane country road, and the refrigerator you bought that was on back order, is still inching along through
that bottleneck." Face it, only a select few of us truly understand logistics, so trying to explain it without the analogy can be futile. But everyone has sat in horrific traffic, trying to squeeze into the narrowest of
roadway funnels. Better yet, that shared experience means that everyone knows firsthand the frustrations and pain points associated with
that bumper-to-bumper nightmare, making the supply-chain woes real
and relatable.

Sometimes analogies can be effective in helping to mitigate a negative perception associated with your company or your industry. A
few years ago, I was helping a sports media company with messaging
on a new product they were launching that would allow viewers to
place bets on the games they were watching. Although more and more
companies have moved into the legalized sports betting category, any
organization that makes wagering more accessible is still going to be
viewed through a controversial lens, given how many people grapple
with the scourge of gambling addiction. The analogy we settled on for
betting on televised sports was "Sports betting is like putting a friendly
wager on a golf match with your friends on a Saturday. Nobody's doing
it to get rich. They're doing it because it boosts their focus and enjoyment and makes them feel more invested in the outcome." If we de-
construct this analogy, a number of things have been worded in a very
intentional way. First, by using golf as the main source of comparison,
we are opting for a venue that has had an extremely long history of betting associated with it. In fact, if you're an adult, I would wager (pardon
the pun) that putting a little money on a golf game might be one of the
only times you place a bet all year, outside of the office pool for your
NCAA bracket or the Super Bowl predict-the-final-score grid.

Describing it as a "friendly" game implies that there's not a large
sum of money riding on the outcome, something "Nobody's doing it
to get rich" also accomplishes. "With your friends on a Saturday" is
meant to conjure up a once-a-week social gathering. The bet seems like

merely an offshoot of that. Stating that wagering "boosts your focus and enjoyment and makes you feel more invested in the outcome" has a double-sided benefit. For the person betting, it's a reminder that when there's some skin in the game, you're likely to concentrate more, and as a result, play better, and who doesn't enjoy playing better? For the media company, this line can reinforce for advertisers that their viewers are more focused on the telecast and more likely to stick with the action, perhaps long after the outcome has been decided.

This strategy of comparing the potentially controversial to the relatively benign is proving to be an effective tactic with firms that need to address the looming threat posed by AI. I am advising my clients to remind their audiences that virtually every technological innovation throughout history has carried with it the fear of devastating disruption. Here are a few:

"When the printing press was first invented, there was vehement opposition because an entire industry of calligraphers was likely to be put out of business. Of course, the number of jobs that the printing press created is immeasurable." Along a similar vein: "When the spreadsheet first came out, people were predicting that accountants would no longer be able to make a living. There are more accountants on the planet today than ever before. Same holds true for the advent of the calculator."

In another messaging session, we used an automobile theme to help respond to critics who express alarm that AI technology is far outpacing the industry's ability to build protective guardrails.

"The early-model automobiles didn't have seat belts, roll bars, anti-lock brakes, or airbags. Those were developed as potential safety issues became apparent."

Last year, a recruiting firm we were working with was also facing a messaging challenge regarding AI. They were deploying it to accelerate and facilitate the process of finding their clients the next big job, but they didn't want the human component of their service to be completely overshadowed. An analogy comparing the job search to another type of challenging quest was where we ultimately landed:

"Finding a top position can feel like climbing a mountain. Standing at the base looking up to the summit can be intimidating. Our firm has always provided the necessary gear for the climb, but now we're equipping you with a sherpa as well, a guide that can help you chart the best course so you can achieve your goal more efficiently."

Recently when working with a venture capital firm that advises founders on how to rapidly scale their companies, the topic of talent came up. It's a widely accepted concept that different stages of a company's growth require different types of talent. The first twenty-five people you hired, who were instrumental in getting the company off the ground, may not be the right people to shepherd you to your Series A funding round. But jettisoning those ground-level loyalists (who likely worked their tails off for you) can seem a bit coldhearted and callous, even though it's the right business decision. This is the perfect job for an analogy.

"You know when you're a little older and you think about the friends you've had since childhood? Sometimes we ask ourselves, would I be friends with this person if I met them today? Often the answer is no. The same dynamic is at play when you evaluate the first twenty-five people you hire at your company."

Using friends and family as the source of the analogy works because just about everyone has both and can therefore relate. So that's the tactic we pursued for a rapidly scaling tech company that found itself at a crossroads. Since its inception, the founder had always dictated product development. But, as in most companies, there comes a time when the founder needs to step back and run the company, handing off the responsibility of product development to a chief product officer. The goal was to be able to explain this inherent tension in a benign way that didn't hint at any friction:

"Tech founders relinquishing product development to a CPO is like having your child go off with the babysitter for the first time. You know it's an important developmental step, but it's never easy."

In 2011, long before Facebook came under fire for its perceived detrimental effects on society, CEO Mark Zuckerberg and COO Sheryl

Sandberg sat down for an interview with disgraced talk-show host Charlie Rose. This was before Facebook was seen as a prime exacerbator of disinformation, fake news, cyberbullying, addictive use, and political polarization. The topic that was problematic for them, even back then, however, was privacy. So when Rose asked Sandberg to respond to critics' concerns, she resorted to the same approach:

"I can remember when caller ID first came out. People were upset, they thought it was an invasion of their privacy to know who was calling. There were calls to regulate it, there were calls to ban it. I don't know anyone today who isn't totally reliant on caller ID."

What made this analogy effective for Sandberg was the attempt to project an outcome for Facebook that mirrored caller ID. Yes, there are concerns now, but over time, those issues will pale in comparison to the enormous functionality of Facebook, just like with caller ID.

During the pandemic, many industries experienced unprecedented disruption, perhaps none more than the spirits industry. In the blink of an eye, the three biggest venues for consumption—bars and restaurants and nightclubs—shuttered. Virtual happy hours caught fire with enjoyment-starved people showcasing their Instagram-worthy homemade cocktails. For the spirits companies, the goal was to inspire people to be their own mixologist, instead of resorting to the ease of opening a beer or a bottle of wine at the end of a grueling day of end-to-end Zoom meetings. So, the analogy that we came up with was:

"Opening a can of beer or a bottle of wine is the equivalent of pulling a frozen pizza out of the freezer for dinner. Mixing a beautiful cocktail is like making a gourmet meal from scratch that impresses your friends."

Like most effective analogies, aspiration resides at its heart. Who doesn't want to be thought of as a culinary creative, whipping up beautiful dinners? There's no imaginative flair needed to untwist a bottle cap or pop open a can. The intention of that analogy was to foster a sense of pride and creativity in showing off your own bartending skills and coax consumers deeper into the cocktail culture. Once that was accomplished, the next task was to use analogy to drive people to a specific brand.

Recently I was helping a well-known premium spirits brand develop messaging around their loss of shelf space in bars, a distribution problem exacerbated by the pandemic. I wanted an analogy that would convey the jarringly unnatural feeling this brand's absence caused:

"Not seeing our brand on the top shelf behind the bar is like seeing a smile that's missing a front tooth," or "A margarita without [Brand X] is like guacamole without chips," or "A margarita without [Brand X] is like a birthday cake without candles."

In spirits, as in many other industries, launching a superpremium product can be a double-edged sword. Innovating and expanding with a luxury offering can elevate the stature of a brand and spark outsize revenue given the higher profit margins it can generate. On the flip side, there is always the risk of cutting into the sales of the existing products in that brand's portfolio, a phenomenon known in the industry as "cannibalizing," a term that goes right up to the line of jargon but stops just shy of crossing it. If there was already an offering that was considered luxury, how do you combat the skeptical perception that maybe it wasn't luxurious enough, if you had to launch something more premium? You need to tout the new kid on the block while preserving the dignity and relevance of the traditional version, a perfect task for a well-conceived analogy:

"You may have two pieces of jewelry from Cartier: a watch that you wear regularly and a bracelet that you don on more special occasions. You love them both equally for how luxurious they feel. The beauty is that there's no need to choose one over the other."

For this particular product launch, here's why that worked. The new champagne is superpremium and from France, so equating it to another luxurious French brand reinforces its elevated stature. The comparison could also have been made to two Hermès scarves. The main point is that this is not an either/or scenario in which you are forced to choose. Both are capable of scratching that luxury itch, just in different ways.

During the pandemic, there was no shortage of medical experts offering their analyses, perspectives, and opinions on the COVID-19 virus. Day after day brought a dizzying array of epidemiologists trying to break down sometimes-complex explanations into simple concepts. Some were more successful than others. The health expert who clearly established himself as a media darling was the head of infectious disease research at the University of Minnesota, Michael Osterholm. He was one of the most sought-after bookings for cable news and national print media alike because of his incredible ability to distill the complex into the accessible and relatable. When the airline mask mandates allowed for passengers to unmask while eating or drinking, Osterholm's analogy crystallized his point of view perfectly:

"A mask mandate with as many exceptions as the airline mandate is like a submarine that closes three of its five doors."

When I saw that quote in the *New York Times*, it was immediately clear to me why his opinion is one of the most coveted in the media.

THE ANALOGY TRIFECTA

Another master of the analogy is Mellody Hobson, whom you met in the last chapter. In a 2020 podcast episode on Goop, Hobson was interviewed about financial empowerment and workplace diversity. Her goal was to make personal investment relatable to an audience primarily focused on issues of personal development, wellness, and lifestyle. Frequently in training sessions, I show video of this interview to demonstrate a perfectly executed analogy, or what we call the "analogy trifecta," because it excels for three reasons: First, the placement of the analogy is perfect. It comes at the end of her answer to a question, which creates the impression that this clever creative device just came to her in the moment. Second, she delivers it with a thoughtful hesitation, as if it's ad-libbed and not practiced several times in front of the mirror. In fact, at the moment of delivery, she breaks eye contact with the interviewer and looks off, as if she's thinking of this in real time. All of this helps create an illusion of spontaneity. Finally, the theme of the analogy is spot-on. She is trying to explain concepts in financial investing to an audience that might feel more at home in a high-end department store than on a trading floor:

"So, we can find investments that are worth a dollar, but we can buy them for sixty cents. That's how we think about it, because that's just the way the world works, people give up on things, stocks get oversold . . . think about it as if you were going to the last call sale at Neiman's—and you could do that all the time. That's what we do, that's what it's like. It's not like some bargain bin, it's like really great things, that are cheap."

Some feel that formulating analogies is not a talent they have in their skill set. Perhaps not. But I *have* seen many clients acquire this ability over time by training their brain to visualize comparisons. Start modestly, focusing on what is familiar to you, and go from there. In the beginning, vet your analogies with a colleague or friend to get an outsider's seal of approval, much like a stand-up comedian might try out jokes on others before adding them to their routine. Feedback from someone whose sensibilities you trust can keep you from falling victim to what we call the dreaded "banalogy," or bad analogy. I'm sure you've seen banalogies on social media that are trite and cringeworthy. One that elicited an audible groan from me the other day was "A bad attitude is like a flat tire. Until you change it, you can't move forward."

Ugh! That makes Forrest Gump's "Life is like a box of chocolates" seem like Shakespeare. Banalogies are proof that sometimes there's a razor-thin line between memorable and moronic, and in a high-stakes arena, that razor's edge can cut deep.

In 2012, Mitt Romney was challenging President Barack Obama's reelection bid. As with most candidates back then, the political rhetoric during the primaries needed to be more staunchly conservative to secure the GOP nomination than it would be in the general election, where conventional wisdom dictates candidates should move their positions and tone toward the middle. Eric Fehrnstrom, Romney's senior campaign adviser, was asked by the press whether the Utah senator's embracing of conservative positions could cost him votes among moderates in November's general election.

"I think you hit a reset button for the fall campaign. Everything changes," Fehrnstrom responded. "It's almost like an Etch A Sketch. You can kind of shake it up, and we start all over again."

Smelling blood, his opponents pounced. Some brought actual Etch A Sketches out on the campaign trail, waving them in the air and declaring, "You have to stand for something that lasts longer than this!" The analogy sure was memorable, but for all the wrong reasons. It became a symbol for Romney's lack of authenticity and conviction, a symbol that he couldn't shake or erase.

My hope is that the examples I've just shared give you a useful framework for you to build your own analogies that hit the bull's-eye and are memorable for all the right reasons.

SUPERSIZE ME

As we discussed in Chapter 2, bringing your analogy into jumbo territory involves creating a longer storytelling version. This can be a highly effective way to begin a keynote presentation. This requires finding a parallel story that shares many of the same characteristics as the topic of your talk. The time-tested success of this type of analogy is in a class by itself. Perhaps the Greatest Story Ever Told wouldn't have been so great had it not been for the jumbo analogy, or as it is referred to in the Bible, a parable. Whether it is the story of the Prodigal Son or the Good Samaritan, the analogous anecdote has been the fuel powering the engine of the world's most populous religion for countless centuries.

Barack Obama was no stranger to the supersized analogy. In a 2022 fundraising speech in New York City, the president wanted to call out the absurd stubbornness of climate change deniers. But getting down into the wonky weeds of climate science is not a great recipe to captivate an audience. So Obama crafted a jumbo analogy that had broad relatability:

"On climate change . . . now [shakes his head in bewilderment]. If you went to a doctor . . . no, let's change that . . . you go to a hundred doctors. And ninety-nine of them tell you, 'You've got diabetes. You've got to stop eating bacon and donuts every day. And we have to monitor your health, and we've got to fix this.' You wouldn't say, 'Aww, that's a conspiracy, they're making that up. All ninety-nine of those doctors got together, with Obama, to try to prevent me from having bacon and donuts. You wouldn't do that!'" The crowd applauded the parallel and heartily laughed, which prompted Obama to add: "I mean, it would be funny, but this is about climate change. This was an analogy."

THE CADILLAC OF ANALOGIES

Last year, a client had a particular challenge facing her in an upcoming town hall at her accounting software company. They had done an admirable job servicing their large enterprise clients as well as their small business clients. Where they had traditionally fallen short was in the midsize market. To correct that deficiency, they tried to jerry-rig their small business product and promote it as a solution for the midmarket, rather than invest the money to make a bespoke offering for that clientele. It failed miserably, and now my trainee was saddled with the responsibility of explaining to the rest of the company why their latest attempt at capturing this coveted market was likely to succeed.

Together we sat down and racked our brains to come up with a historical parallel that would put their strategic mistake in context and project a positive outcome. What we came up with was a story that harked back to 1984 Detroit and one of the biggest automotive industry blunders since the catastrophic failure of a model called the Edsel. It went something like this:

In 1982, Cadillac wanted to capture the middle-class car buyer who aspired to own a Cadillac. The model they built was called the Cadillac Cimarron. On paper it sounded like a good idea, but it turned into a debacle that damaged one of Detroit's most iconic luxury brands. What they should have done was build a new car from scratch. But they thought they could take a shortcut and merely add some quasi-luxury touches to the down-market Chevy Nova and pass it off as a Cadillac. It was a colossal failure. The consumer, whom they clearly underestimated, saw right through it. The historic blunder, however, did lead to something spectacular. Acknowledging the value of creating something genuinely new, GM created not just a new model, but a whole new category: luxury SUVs. The Cadillac Escalade was the phoenix that rose out of the ashes of the Cimarron. It was a megasuccess, undoing the damage done by the Cimarron and then some.

Now comes the most crucial part of any jumbo analogy you're using to begin a talk, the connective tissue to the topic you're addressing. Without this, a story is just a story. The connector drives the point home and gives the story relevant meaning.

"We've all endured our own Cimarron miscue. Now it's our turn to have our Escalade moment. Like GM, we're about to prove that mistakes can lead to something brand-new and something great." Think of this technique as projection through reflection.

Marc Jones, the chief technical officer of Alkami, demonstrated a captivating use of the jumbo analogy in a talk he gave at the Co:lab conference in 2022. He began with a super-simple slide in an enormous font that said: "4:00."

He didn't begin with an agenda and he didn't succumb to talking about what he was going to talk about. Instead, he dove right in:

"On May sixth, 1954, history was made as Roger Bannister became the first person to break the four-minute mile. Now, the story has become legendary, since before Bannister, physiologists had long thought that running a four-minute mile was impossible, if not potentially deadly. And even if you know this story, you may not know all of it."

When I have recommended this type of start to clients, I often hear "Starting off with something seemingly so random, isn't that going to confuse the audience? Aren't they going to wonder how I'm going to get from there to the topic of my presentation?" "Yes!" I tell them. Inviting the audience to figure out how you're going to connect the dots is a form of engagement. In fact, it's more likely to immerse them in the storytelling and make them listen more closely.

In the last line to that opening paragraph, Jones was strategically clever in teasing his intention of revealing an element to the story of which many are unaware. A simple line like this may at first glance seem like a throwaway, but it is deliberately inserted to heighten the audience's curiosity. For the next minute or so, Jones gets into the details of Bannister's plan to achieve his goal, how, together with his team, Bannister made adjustments to his training regimen, his running style, and even the construction of his running shoes, all in an effort to maximize his speed.

On its own, it is an interesting historical tale. But without the connective tissue, it's merely a random story that *will* leave the audience bewildered as to its significance. Jones, however, ties it all together:

"Now, Bannister's story proves the impossible is possible with the right ingredients: vision, preparation, and collaboration. And I have the privilege of speaking with digital and technology leaders across our client base regularly, and each has a vision for where they want to take their FI (financial institution). They have planned for success, and they recognize they can't go it alone if they are to cross the finish line and set a new bar for themselves."

By extending the metaphor beyond the story in this connective paragraph with "finish line" and "setting a new bar," Jones makes the beginning feel expertly crafted. Now that he has their attention, he is free to take the talk anywhere he chooses.

METAPHOR

Given that a metaphor is a colorful comparative device as well, you can think of it as a first cousin to the analogy. When poet laureate Amanda Gorman sat down for an interview with Trevor Noah in 2021, she was fresh off delivering her captivating poem "The Hill We

Climb" at President Joe Biden's inauguration. Just two weeks earlier, on January 6, a violent mob had stormed the U.S. Capitol to prevent members of the House from certifying the results of the 2020 election. The role her poem played in helping to neutralize the stench of that shameful episode was the point she made so beautifully through the use of metaphor:

"I think a lot of times in cultures, we often think of ways that we can cleanse ourselves with water. I think of the ways that we can cleanse ourselves with words, meaning that this poem was an opportunity to kind of resanctify, repurify, and reclaim, not just the Capitol Building, but American democracy and what it stands for."

What stood out from that interview was Noah's visible reaction to Gorman's metaphor. The angle of his head rose, as did his eyebrows, sharing an audible "Hmmm," as if to say, "That's certainly an interesting way of thinking about it!" If Noah remembers anything from that conversation, I'm sure it's that.

A few years ago, at an Investor Day conference for a hedge fund, a group of economic experts were assembled for a panel discussion on Brexit. On the "Scintillating Scale," Brexit is just slightly below supply chains and the insurance industry. Show me a conversation dedicated to Brexit and I'll show you a destination for Morpheus (the god of sleep) to swoop down and claim as many victims as possible. But on this occasion, one of the panelists said something that has stuck with me to this day:

"Listen, let's face it. Before Theresa May left office as the prime minister of the U.K., she was the chess player who only had the king left. And she was just moving it around one space at a time until she was checkmated."

I don't remember anyone else who was on that panel that day, I don't remember what anyone else on that panel said that day, but I remember that guy. His metaphor stuck.

When President Joe Biden stumbled badly in the first debate of the 2024 election season, many called for him to step aside in favor of a younger candidate. Most of the statements sounded about the same, except for the metaphor offered by Poland's foreign minister, who expressed concern that Biden's approach to succession planning made media mogul Logan Roy's in the show *Succession* seem neat and orderly: "It's important to manage one's ride into the sunset."

On the subject of AI, a client and I were working on messaging to try to convey that they were building the technology in a responsible way but not so timidly that the opportunities for breakthrough innovation would be stifled. The metaphor we arrived at: "We're building it with guardrails but we're not fitting it with a straitjacket."

Jeremy Stoppelman, the CEO and cofounder of Yelp, knows how to wield a metaphor to help explain the problem his company is solving. In a 2014 interview on NPR's *Marketplace*, host Kai Ryssdal asked about the big knock on Yelp, that a couple of bad reviews could doom a business. Stoppelman responded:

"If you think about the world prior to Yelp, it was the world of the professional critic, and so that meant lots of businesses didn't get any exposure at all, and the ones that did had kind of a one-shot deal where a supposed expert, they would come a few times to the restaurant and then that was the reputation of the restaurant. And the beauty of Yelp is that it's now this *concert of opinions*, where every day there are new customers coming in and there's new opportunities to give them a great experience and earn yourself a great review."

It's not an accident, nor is it a coincidence, that Stoppelman reserves the memorable metaphor for highlighting his company's solution. That's what he wants to have stick. I've had people remark, "There's no way he came up with that on the spot. I'm sure he's said that a million times," to which I say, "And the problem with that is?"

It makes no sense to go to all the hard work of crafting a clever metaphor or analogy, only to throw it away after just one use. But therein lies a trap that I often have seen very intelligent people fall into: thinking that reusing a turn of phrase is somehow cheesy. "Oh, I can't say that again, I said it last time." I urge you to be more creatively sustainable in your approach. Scrap the one-and-done mindset. Do you think comedians feel any sense of shame telling the same joke to different audiences? If they did, they would exhaust their material after just a couple of performances. Also keep in mind that if you've come up with something really good, people will enjoy hearing it again. Adam Grant, the behavioral psychologist, has a great point of view on repeating yourself: "Good communication requires repetition. When you're tired of your messages, it's just starting to land."

CREATIVE LABEL

If you're a fan of Larry David, whether it be *Curb Your Enthusiasm* or *Seinfeld*, you are well acquainted with creative labels. Of all the comedic devices he has wielded over the years, these are by far the stickiest:

Sample Abuse
Stop and Chat
Side Sitting
Verbal Texting
Social Assassin

And my personal favorite, the Big Goodbye. By now I'm sure you've deduced that a creative label is an expression you coin that succinctly describes a social phenomenon or personal characteristic. For Larry, the Big Goodbye is his patented technique for avoiding someone at a party but pretending that's not what you were doing:

You avoid a person all night and then when it's time to leave, you go, "Hey!" and you give 'em a big goodbye and they feel good, they're very happy that you spent this time with them at the end of the night and then you slip out.

I probably have Larry to thank for being the inspiration behind a creative label developed in a messaging session with one of the major streaming entertainment companies. We were addressing the industry problem of new subscribers consuming all the content they want on the platform and then promptly discontinuing their subscription, a phenomenon we called "binge and drop."

Entire periods of economic activity have been characterized by attaching a creative label. In 1996, the chairman of the Federal Reserve Board, Alan Greenspan, used the term "irrational exuberance" to characterize unjustifiably high prices for stocks and other assets. The term took on a life of its own, unlike the title of his speech: "The Challenge of Central Banking in a Democratic Society" (yawn!). Perhaps because economic theory can be a tad dry now and then, these labels have helped liven up the discourse. In 1992, economist David Shulman was widely credited with coming up with the label "Goldilocks economy" to describe the economy as not being too hot or too cold, but "just right."

I've come across many over the years that are worthy of a sticky place in our memories. During a training session with notable New York sleep doctor Qanta Ahmed, I asked out of curiosity whether there really were high-performance executives who only need three or four hours of sleep, or who can regularly pull all-nighters. "That's nonsense," she said. "Everyone needs a solid six to eight hours a night. Anyone claiming otherwise is engaging in 'sleep machismo.'" It's been over fifteen years since she said that to me, yet I still remember it and credit her for having come up with it.

Since Dr. Ahmed's position has been widely endorsed throughout the medical community and beyond as a critical component of wellness, it's now trendy for corner-office occupants to claim that they adhere to a strict eight hours of sleep. Perhaps we should now call them ZzzzzzEOs.

WHEN GOOD LABELS GO BAD

The memorable nature of creative labels makes misfiring with them wildly problematic, because like the banalogy, if you get it wrong, it will take longer for your mistake to fade from people's minds. It's a lesson that Hillary Clinton learned the hard way when her own Etch A Sketch moment damaged her chances to become president.

It happened at a glitzy fundraiser in September 2016 at an upscale New York restaurant. "I am all that stands between you and the apocalypse," she told the adoring and cheering crowd. She talked about all the "deplorable" qualities that defined her opponent, Donald Trump, and all the terrible consequences that electing him would bring. She would have been well advised to stop there, but she decided to go for more. "You could put half of Trump's supporters into what I call the *basket of deplorables.* Right?"

It was a creative label that turned into a corrosive faux pas.

The remark might have been red meat to the crowd, but it left a sour taste in a lot of people's mouths, a critical mistake that cost her dearly just eight weeks before election day. For Clinton, an experienced campaigner and politician, it was a rookie mistake—you can criticize your opponent to your heart's content, but never take shots at voters.

The postelection analysis proved how costly the ad lib was. Diane Hessan, a consultant to Hillary, offered a fresh perspective in an article in the *Boston Globe*, saying that she tracked undecided voters to assess their reaction to the term "deplorable." It turned out it was more strongly negative than the flap over Clinton's private email server or FBI director James B. Comey's comments about the emails. "There was one moment when I saw more undecided voters shift to Trump than any other, when it all changed, when voters began to speak differently about their choice," she wrote.

Creative labels have been used to define historical groups. Those who fought and defeated fascism in World War II have been called the "Greatest Generation," and sadly, many have labeled Generation Z the "Loneliest Generation," due to the degree in which virtual connections through social media have superseded real, in-person relationships.

I maintain that one of the most consequential domestic policies in Europe over the past twenty-five years would not have received the global attention it did had it not been for the clever and catchy label of "Brexit." I doubt it would have been the subject of intense debate in pubs all over Britain had it been described as "the U.K.'s departure from the European Union." When Prince Harry and his wife, Meghan Markle, opted to separate from the British royal family in 2020, another creative label was born: "Megxit."

Entire industries have been created on the backs of creative labels. Case in point? The "home edit." This was a basic household organizational idea that was perceived as a transformational concept mainly based on an original label. Years earlier, I became a devotee of displaying pantry items in clear, glass jars to which I attached labels. When the home edit became all the rage for how to organize your kitchen, advocating many of the same ideas, my niece Emily looked around my kitchen and incredulously said, "They have some nerve calling that *home edit* new! You've been doing this for years!" Now it seems that when any retail company wants to sell something they call it "shoe edit" or "handbag edit." There's a podcast called *The Wellness Edit*. Can the "steel-belted radial tire edit" be far behind? But that is the American way. Take an idea that has caught on and imitate it to the point where you've squeezed out every last ounce of life.

Consumer packaged goods companies unwittingly gave rise to the creative label "shrinkflation" when they began charging the same amount of money for smaller packages containing less product. I remember seeing the term on CNBC in 2023, but it only really became part of the national vernacular when Cookie Monster publicly decried the practice on X: "Me hate shrinkflation. Me cookies are getting smaller!"

That led to one of the best viral buzzes possible, with President Biden crediting Cookie Monster in his State of the Union address for spotting and calling out this brand of corporate greed: "A bag of chips has fewer chips, but they're still charging us just as much."

Since then, the concept keeps rising up the political agenda in the U.S., undoubtedly in no small part due to the imagery this catchy term easily conjures up. Interestingly, shrinkflation's first cousin, "greedflation," was added to Dictionary.com. If you followed the conversations coming out of the World Economic Forum in Davos, Switzerland, in 2024, you also would have come across "skimpflation." This is the phenomenon in which corporations cut back, not on the quantity, but on the quality of the product, meaning that your chicken enchilada product suddenly contains less chicken. All these phenomena can create what's called a "vibecession," in which the economy is strong on paper but people aren't feeling good about their own situations.

"'Vibecession' was brilliant," said Stephanie Ruhle. "It captured exactly what we were feeling. It might not be a recession, but man, when everything you do costs more, it just feels shitty."

Perhaps you've never been aware that these clever and memorable devices all fall under the same category, but I guarantee you, now you will notice them all around you.

Great Resignation	The pandemic-era trend of workers reevaluating their careers and leaving their jobs
Quiet Quitting	When employees give the minimum effort to keep their jobs but don't go the extra mile for their employer
Toothbrush Test	Google cofounder Larry Page's barometer for how successful a company is likely to be—use it once or twice a day
Greenwashing	When a company misleads you into thinking they're more environmentally conscious than they really are
Seesaw Economy, or the Optimism Lag	When economic indicators are all pointing in a positive direction but consumer confidence is trending down, aka the aforementioned "vibecession"
Slide Karaoke	The style of presenting in which every word on the slide is read by the presenter
Bullhorn Luxury	The antonym for "quiet luxury" that refers to people who ostentatiously display their wealth

FOUR-STAR CLEVERNESS

One of the most clever and memorable lines ever delivered by a public figure combined an analogy with a creative label, a double bang-for-the-buck quote. It's attributed to the late secretary of state Colin Powell. In 2004, Powell was discussing the cautious way the United States should think about contributing to the demise of any dictator, whether it be Assad(s) in Syria or Hussein in Iraq, for fear of what could fill the power vacuum your actions create. Unlike most career diplomats, who might have been prone to prattling on about the intricacies of regime change in the Middle East, Powell made his message succinct and highly relatable. He said, "This is the Pottery Barn Rule. If you break it, you own it," meaning that if you precipitate the demise of a despot, you are now responsible for the hopes, aspirations, and problems of the people of that country. What makes it brilliant is its universal meaning. Not many people easily embrace foreign policy doctrine, but everyone gets that when you walk into a store and knock something over, you have to pay for it. And to this day, the Pottery Barn Rule is still talked about in discussions on international affairs.

TWISTED CLICHÉ

When I was very young, I subscribed to *Sports Illustrated*, and a headline for one of their articles has stuck with me throughout these many years. If you saw the 2017 film *Battle of the Sexes*, starring Emma Stone and Steve Carell, you'll be familiar with this story.

Bobby Riggs, a professional tennis player who won the singles, doubles, and mixed doubles titles at Wimbledon all in the same year (1939), reinvented himself in the 1970s as a brash, misogynistic, carnival-barking tennis hustler who challenged the top women on the tennis tour to a match. In 1973 he took on Australia's Margaret Court, the No. 1 player at the time on the women's circuit. She was thirty, he was fifty-five. The match was ironically played on Mother's Day, with Riggs, ever the showman and applier of psychological pressure, presenting his opponent with a bouquet of roses on the court before they began. To many people's astonishment, Court got crushed 6–2, 6–1. The majority of the headlines that day screamed "Mother's Day Massacre." That's way too forgettable as far as I'm concerned. The *Sports Illustrated* headline, however, stuck: "Mother's Day Ms.-match." That was my first exposure to what I call a "twisted cliché" and I've been a rabid fan of them ever since.

You create a twisted cliché by taking a cliché, word, or well-known expression and giving it a twist to create something that sounds very similar but is new and different. In the case of the Riggs-Court headline, "mismatch" became "Ms.-match." Super clever!

I never, ever thought that any type of cliché would be something to aspire to. All clichés do is make people sound like everyone else, which makes it impossible to stand out. But I love when they get twisted because it creates the unexpected. They stop you dead in your tracks for a split second trying to figure out what it is that's slightly off. However, a word of caution here is important. Don't make your twisted cliché so obscure that your audience needs more than a beat to process it. The New York tabloid newspapers, the *Daily News* and the *New York Post*, employ this device nearly every day, especially on the back sports-page headline.

I love this device so much that I considered using it for the title of this book. My thought was calling it "Puttin' on the Rizz: How to Dazzle People When You Speak." As much as I liked flipping the song title "Puttin' on the Ritz" by substituting "Ritz" with the more contemporary "Rizz" (short for charisma or style), the play on words must work on both ends of the twist. The song was written by Irving Berlin in 1927, and although it's been revived a few times, it's old! "Rizz" is a term popularized by YouTuber Kai Cenat in 2021, so expecting people to make the leap from Berlin to Cenat is a tall ask. Someone is destined to be left out of the joke, and that is not an option.

While working with one of Silicon Valley's venture capital firms, we wanted to make the point that 2021 saw a massive influx of novice investors throwing seed-stage money at any startup that sounded even mildly compelling. We wanted to make the point memorable, so we called the phenomenon a "seeding frenzy."

We also wanted to emphasize how substantially New York City had grown as a hub for new tech firms. The challenge there was just the overwhelming number of directions in which to possibly go, given how many different clichés describe New York. We finally settled on: "The city that never sleeps is a great place for founders who never rest." In this instance, you leave the actual cliché alone, and instead you annex it with a line that resembles it in sound and structure but is different. A similar approach worked to help us explain a classic trap for tech entrepreneurs: spending years building a company that provides a solution to a problem nobody really cares about. For this, we went outside the world of tech and referenced the most famous line from the 1989 film *Field of Dreams*: "If you build it, they will come. Great movie, bad advice."

For a company whose technology makes apps on your phone load faster, we were messaging about consumer impatience, and how it climbs to a whole new level when you have to wait more than a beat. If it takes too long, people will abandon you and go on to the next app. For this, Charles Darwin seemed an appropriate target of our twist: "The competitive landscape is a 'survival of the quickest' scenario." Just swapping out "fittest" with "quickest" gets the job done.

If the twist can be accomplished in just one word, then you have an even more effective device that is a hybrid of a twisted cliché and a creative label. In trying to explain that the rum category was having a moment, somewhat like gin had recently, we coined the term "rumassaince." The entire story of the 2023 Hollywood box office can also be summed up in one word: "Barbenheimer." This blending of two words to make a new word is also called a "portmanteau."

WORDPLAY

The fifth of the Magnificent Seven, which piques our attention and sticks in our brains, is wordplay, the juxtaposition of complementary or contrasting words or concepts. Michelle Obama did it simply and brilliantly in 2016 at the Democratic National Convention when addressing the Republican nominee's brass-knuckles campaigning style: "When someone is cruel or acts like a bully, you don't stoop to their level. No, our motto is: 'When they go low, we go high.'"

One of the most memorable lines from Martin Luther King Jr.'s famed "I Have a Dream" speech has wordplay: "I have a dream that my four little children will one day live in a nation where they will not be judged by the color of their skin, but by the content of their character."

While we were helping a group of venture capitalists from India explain the premium that consumers in India place on quality, this was the line that originally appeared in the presenter's notes: "Consumers are always skeptical, and that concern about quality enters into nearly every purchase they make, from food at the grocery store to the biggest-ticket items." A simple wordplay transformed that thought into something stickier: "In India, consumers are rightly skeptical. Concern about quality doesn't matter, whether you're buying tomatoes or purchasing a car that could turn out to be a lemon."

Any efforts that can keep you away from the tired old cliché "We take this problem very, very seriously" is a noble cause. When it comes to thorny topics, corporations lean on this phrase so heavily that it has come to mean absolutely nothing, a line that has an empty, obligatory feel to it. Beverage alcohol companies have used it for years: "We take responsible drinking very, very seriously." Social media companies resort to it as well: "We take disinformation on our platform very, very seriously." Tech companies are guilty of it when talking about safeguarding user data: "We take data security very, very seriously." A simple wordplay could give a fresh sound to a company's expression of concern and commitment to tackling a persistent problem: "Data security is our top priority and our bottom line."

In the belief that you can never have enough fresh messaging when it comes to AI, a couple of turns of phrase come to mind. Skepticism abounds that this technology will play a major role in people losing their jobs to increased automation. The counterargument is that AI will merely be a valuable assistant to us, performing tasks that are either boringly repetitive or too massive in scale for any human being to handle. This, we're told, will free us up to take on more satisfying and challenging assignments. That was the inspiration behind "It's hard to move your company forward when you're mired in the back office."

The wordplay with AI doesn't get any simpler or succinct than "less mundane, more rewarding." Besides its brevity, there's another reason why I like this one. It mimics one of the most successful ad-campaign slogans of all time, Miller Lite beer's "tastes great, less filling." Anytime you can mirror, but not copy, the sound, structure, or style of a line that has been emblazoned into our memories, you benefit from the familiarity of it. The same dynamics were at play with a line I recommended to another client that had a retail location considered to be a "must" destination in the heart of New York City. For the sake of this example, we'll call the brand "Richardson's." The suggested line was "Oh, everybody comes to Richardson's," which mimics a line from the iconic film *Casablanca*, in which Captain Renault says to Major Strasser, "Oh, everybody comes to Rick's," referring to the café owned by Humphrey Bogart's character. I wasn't expecting anyone to actually place where they'd heard a similar line before, but there's value in having them recognize its familiarity, even if it's on a subconscious level.

Another example of wordplay on the promise of AI alleviating the oppressiveness of tedious work? "I love my job, but I hate my day." Like AI, cybersecurity can be another subject that's conceptually hard to get our arms around, and the more obscure the topic, the greater the need for punchy ways to talk about it. In discussing the critical importance of a company being 100 percent airtight in thwarting bad actors from wreaking havoc through a cyberattack, the line we liked was "Great isn't good enough, when what you need is perfect." The proximity of those three words—"Great," "good," and "perfect"—makes this more memorable than merely saying, "It only takes one attack to go undefended for big problems to arise." Another wordplay to convey the growing sophistication of cyberattackers: "Hackers don't break in, they log in."

Early in 2019, I was having a drink with Paul Begala, who had been an adviser to Bill Clinton and a CNN political pundit. At the time, everyone was wondering if Donald Trump really stood a chance of winning a second time. Most thought his chances were slim at best, but Begala said something that night I remember to this day: "Strong and wrong always beats right and weak." He wasn't saying Trump was strong, but the image producer Mark Burnett created in the character Trump played on *The Apprentice* projected strength and decisiveness, and in his mind, that could be enough to win.

The memorable nature of wordplay stems from the lyrical sound that's created when either similar or contrasting words are placed close together. In my work with legendary Wall Street executive Patricia Chadwick, who authored the book *Breaking Glass: Tales from the Witch of Wall Street*, we wanted to pick up on the "witch" imagery while conveying the idea that one of the keys to her success was her willingness to take on any project where she could show her value. "I wasn't waving some magic wand around, but my hand *was* always in the air volunteering for projects."

A few other generic wordplays for business, with terms that play off each other italicized:

PHRASE	OFFSETTING WORDS
"She's an *incredible* woman, doing *remarkable* things."	"incredible"—"remarkable"
"We're tapping into the *depths* of our *insights* and the *breadth* of our *experience*."	"depths"—"breadth" "insights"—"experience"
"It's better to *speak thoughtfully* than to *recite robotically*."	"speak"—"recite" "thoughtfully"—"robotically"
"*Quiet* quitting has become a *loud* fizzle."	"quiet"—"loud"

DATA WITH CONTEXT

"Data is the new oil" may be an old analogy, but it keeps getting more apt all the time. It has been the driver of corporate analytics and insights for many years, but with the advent of generative AI, it has attained an even loftier perch of importance. That's because without the data put into it, today's large language model is like a top-of-the-line electric vehicle (EV) without a lithium-ion battery. It just kind of sits there. This has sparked an intense infatuation with using data in our presentations, reams and reams of data. I have heard more than my share of presentations that cough up clusters of data points in such a dense and concentrated way that I feel lightheaded and dizzy from the statistical assault.

FIRE UP THE POPCORN

Ironically, when it comes to communicating in a memorable way, data alone is that EV without the battery. What propels the data forward in the recesses of our minds is context. In real, everyday terms, what does that data point mean? In my work with one of the major wireless carrier networks, the messaging leaned heavily on their 5G achieving speeds of 100 megabits per second, something they proudly repeated multiple times. The toughest part of my job is confessing ignorance in the face of industry knowledge or terminology, but I had no option other than to say, "One hundred mbps? Is that good?"

"Oh yes," they reassured me, "it's the new industry standard."

"Okay, well then, we need to illustrate why that speed is important. Put that into some kind of context," I said. "Practically, what can I do with that connection speed?"

"It means you can download a high-definition movie in about three minutes," they explained.

Ah! Now we were onto something. From there we were able to attach an experiential component to the data point. My recommendation was to say, "In the time it takes for you to go to the kitchen and microwave the popcorn, your hi-def movie is ready to watch." After all, that's the only thing that really matters to people.

Renewable-energy companies also speak in abstract data points, which makes it nearly impossible for the average person to fully comprehend the environmental benefit behind the transition away from fossil fuels. One particular company I worked with is the driving force behind a windmill project off the eastern seaboard of the United States. Their messaging focused on the total amount of power this installation will generate, and they conveyed that simply through a data point: 1,870 megawatts. Confession time again!

"I'm sorry, but I'm a little rusty on my megawatt conversion tables these days," I said. "I'm sure that number is meant to impress me, and I'm sure I will be if you can tell me what that means in practical terms."

"Well, think of it this way. It's enough wind power to light one million homes."

"That *is* a big deal," I admitted. "And I would imagine that there's two sides to this green coin. What the generated power does, but also the amount of carbon people will not be generating thanks to this sustainable alternative. Before you reply with just data, think what is the tangible, relatable equivalent? Because when you're up in front of an audience giving a presentation, no one is likely to interrupt you and ask you to put that into context for them. You need to proactively provide that if you want to keep them captivated."

"It's enough power to reduce emissions by nearly four million U.S. tons," the executive replied.

We were getting closer, but we weren't there yet.

"Good! But if I'm not familiar with what the weight of carbon means, how do you get me to care about this?" I asked.

"Imagine saving enough carbon emissions that it would be equivalent to taking 700,000 cars off the road annually."

Message accomplished! This level of understanding goes beyond this executive being more memorable and getting engagement and retention from his audience. If he was pitching this project to a state power authority or a regulatory agency, it could mean the difference between getting buy-in for the project or getting it mothballed.

SPICING UP THE DATA

As invigorating as it is to help young brands and startup companies get grooved in their messaging, there's also something thrilling about working with brands that have attained an iconic status over the course of decades, or in some cases a century or more. Tabasco is one of those legendary American companies that since the nineteenth century has established an astonishing global reach. You can find their hot sauce (technically it's called "pepper sauce") in 195 countries, which prompted me to ask in a recent messaging session how many bottles they make on a daily basis.

"Seven hundred thousand!" said Harold "Tuck" Osborn, the CEO.

"Holy habañero! That's a lot of hot sauce!" I said. "I think sometimes people have a hard time visualizing how big a number that really is. I wonder if we can put that in the context it deserves."

"Well," said Tuck, "you would need two full-sized tractor-trailer trucks to distribute it from our facility in Avery Island, Louisiana."

"That's a pretty impressive visual," I agreed. "But we're all foodies here, right? I want your product to be visualized in its proper setting. I think we all agree that there's nothing about an eighteen-wheeler that makes my mouth water."

So, we brainstormed a bit over our morning bagels and cream cheese that, yes, of course, had a healthy sprinkling of their hero-product, classic red sauce. (Hey, don't knock it unless you've tried it!)

We agreed that beyond our own kitchen cupboard or pantry, the most synonymous setting for a Tabasco bottle was a table in a restaurant, particularly a diner. So we looked up how many diners there are in the United States: almost 10,000. Then we tried to get a fix on the average number of tables in a classic dinner: around 20. So we dusted off our basic math skills and multiplied 20 by 10,000 (200,000) to find out the total number of tables. We then divided that into the total number of Tabasco bottles produced every day (700,000) and what we get is a data point with context we all like. Put simply, here's how it sounds:

"We make enough Tabasco every day to put more than three bottles on every table in every diner in America."

We live in a time in which we are searching for the harmonious balance between humans and machines. Nothing good comes from that balance getting thrown out of whack (more about that in Chapter 14), especially when it comes to communication. Data, for data's sake, doesn't do the job. Humanizing it with engaging, relatable, and visual context supercharges the data's impact and makes it more memorable.

ORIGINAL DEFINITIONS

Throughout this book, I take corporate buzzwords to task, and for good reason. That's because when they get repeated, the fuzzier their meaning becomes, and the greater the need for them to have a clear and succinct definition. Even simple words like "energy" are so broad as to need specific-use clarification. Perhaps you've received some feedback on your presentation-delivery style over the course of your career and that word has crept into the critique: "That was a solid presentation, but next time maybe bring a little more energy." TV news journalists, who do their reporting on camera, often get told that by executives in charge. "Where's the energy? I didn't see that energy tonight!"

When I did that for a living in a previous career, I was always left wondering, "What do they mean by 'energy'? Do they mean I should start flailing my arms, talk more with my hands, speak louder, speak faster?" No one ever answered that question. It's only after two decades of coaching people to better captivate an audience that I've arrived at the most practical and targeted definition of what "energy" in the context of public speaking really means.

"Energy is your visible enthusiasm for the value of the information you're sharing."

I've shared that definition with thousands of people because, early on, I realized that it connected with people. They remembered it. There's something about framing information in the form of a definition that is sticky for people. Since then, I've encouraged the people I train to incorporate an original definition into their scripts and presenter's notes when appropriate. Here's what I mean by "original." It is *not* the definition you would find in the dictionary, but rather a complementary meaning that helps you emphasize one of your points.

For instance, for a consumer goods company that was changing the look of their product, the word "packaging" came up frequently. If you look up that word in *Webster's*, you'll find this: "materials used to wrap or protect products." Together we crafted a more original definition that incorporated an element of emotion:

"Packaging is the first impression you create with your customer."

That teed up the following sentence, which spoke to how crucial it is to execute flawlessly: "And we all know that you don't get a second chance to get that right."

The notion of "bringing value" is a universal business imperative for companies in every industry and geography, yet the concept can be a bit opaque when I ask people to explain what they mean. The *Oxford English Dictionary* defines value as "the regard that something is held to deserve; the importance, worth or usefulness of something." I prefer a more practical, tangible, and relatable definition: "Value is the distance between what someone expects from you and what you actually deliver." A client of ours said that at a recent conference and got a lot of tweets quoting them.

A big component of value is customer service and how I, as a consumer, feel catered to. There are many different ways to demonstrate this, but one that I love, given the attention-challenged and distracted world in which we live, is "The height of customer service is giving someone your complete and undivided attention."

If you're a leader in business and you're urged to demonstrate "authenticity," looking it up in the dictionary won't be very helpful. There you'll find: "The quality of being legitimate, real or true." That may explain the "what," but it doesn't really articulate the "how." How do I go about projecting authenticity? The simplest definition I've been able to formulate that seems to be striking a relatable chord with clients is "Authenticity = Passion + Warmth."

MATHEMATICAL EQUATIONS

I love segues, and the last of our original definitions gives me the perfect opportunity to deploy one, because the definition of authenticity also belongs to the last of our Magnificent Seven: Mathematical Equations. Now, if math wasn't your thing in school—I can relate—don't worry. You don't need any algebra or trigonometry prowess to make math work for you in your quest to be a more memorable speaker. In fact, it may be one of the rare instances when math and English come together to form a powerful tag team. A mathematical equation can be either an equation using addition, like in the above definition of authenticity, or a ratio, like "the more memorable your communication, the more impact you have." It's typically a statement of cause and effect that requires hyperbrevity, so by its very nature it's punchy. Here are a few examples of mathematical equations that have been used to make bland, corporate messaging come to life:

ORIGINAL STATEMENT	STATEMENT USING MATH
It's important to be projecting a casual and conversational presenting style to create the impression that you're in command of the stage.	The more casual and conversational your tone, the more confident and capable you'll seem.
Organizations today benefit from displaying a strong and authentic commitment to DEI. If everyone in the room comes from the same background and experience, you're at a strategic disadvantage when it comes to developing solutions to problems.	The more diverse your organization, the more comprehensive your creative problem-solving abilities.
Leaders today need to possess a set of qualities and characteristics that makes them models of inspiration for those who work for them. They also need to demonstrate a strong degree of certainty in their vision to motivate and inspire people who feel the leader connects with them and understands them.	Leadership = Empathy + a Vision Driven by Conviction + Inspiration.

Besides their punchy and concise nature, I wasn't completely sure why these equations were such an effective communication tool. Then I had the pleasure of working with Shalinee Sharma, the founder and CEO of the nation's most prominent organization for math learning, Zearn. During the course of our session, she said something that made me realize why mathematical equations work.

"In a world where finding truth can be increasingly elusive, math represents one of the last great sources of truth." That was it! Mathematics fosters a sense of absolute certainty. There can be many different ways of finding an answer, but in math, only one answer can be true. Conviction in our vision, our point of view, and our purpose is a huge component of effective and memorable communication. By presenting our thoughts in a mathematical framework, we benefit from that air of certainty.

A modern-day master of the memorable line is Airbnb CEO Brian Chesky. Brian pays close attention to which parts of his narrative work best and are memorable to people and, following Adam Grant's advice, he is not reluctant to repurpose them, especially if he's playing to different audiences. At a 2022 tech conference, he sat down for a fireside chat with Kara Swisher to discuss the social impacts of COVID. He wanted to make the point that one of the greatest dangers facing us coming out of the pandemic was loneliness. In observing our growing state of isolation, he could have said, "What we're seeing now is a host of activities that have traditionally been done externally in the company of others, to now a more internal, individual dynamic at home." That would have been pretty dull and forgettable. So instead he delivered a soundbite that stuck with the audience: "The mall is now Amazon, the theater is now Netflix, and the office is now Zoom." Scores of people in attendance tweeted that out, creating a viral appreciation for the way Brian took an observation, one that others have likely made, and elevated his to the top of the memorable category, all because of his rapid-fire analogy trifecta. A few weeks later, while being interviewed on a CNN morning news program, Brian went back to that greatest hit and said the exact same thing. The lesson here? Get some mileage out of your memorable content.

I certainly don't expect you to indulge in all seven of these magnificent devices. Some will naturally come more easily to you than others. But I guarantee you that the next time you listen to someone speak, and a compelling and thought-provoking line sticks with you long past the conclusion of the speech or presentation, it will be because one of these techniques has been deployed. There's also a high probability that your audience has never heard this said in any previous presentation, which is a huge asset. Because as we'll discover in the next chapter, a lack of originality is a surefire way to be forgettable.

DO THIS	NOT THAT
Plan Clever, Memorable Lines in Advance	Try to Be Spontaneously Clever
Begin with Jumbo Analogy Storytelling	Begin by Setting the Agenda
Vet Clever Lines with Someone You Trust	Road Test Your Lines with Real Audiences
Ensure Analogies Are Culturally Relevant	Use Obscure Cultural References

6

THE CONFORMITY TRAP

JARGON AND CLICHÉ

"From an oration perspective, the best way to unpack an eradification of your jargon journey is to double down on decomplexifying what you're uttering from a content standpoint."

I was walking to our Rockefeller Center offices one morning in mid-town Manhattan when I spotted the height of jargon absurdity: a sign on an office building offering leased space on Madison Avenue touting the property's "iconicicity." I had to do a double take. *Iconicicity?* I know "iconicity" is a word, albeit an obscure one, but "iconicicity" had me opening my dictionary app to see if it was legitimate. As I suspected, there is no such word. Even if the owners had the best office space in New York, on principle I would never lease there. That's how vehemently opposed I am to jargon.

I find it incongruous that in this era of authenticity (which at some point in the future will no doubt be changed to authenticicity) there hasn't been all-out war declared on jargon. Authenticity, as we define it in Chapter 5, is passion plus warmth. There is nothing warm about jargon. It creates a distant, cold barrier between you and your audience. Jargon is a mask people hide behind that denies others access to who we really are. So, if you're prone to speaking in jargon, peel off that mask.

As a concept, there's lip service paid in some companies to how detrimental jargon is to how we communicate, but when I hear people use it in the workplace, nobody seems to get called on it. That's *my* job. When I find myself barraged with jargon, one of the things I constantly hear myself ask is, "What are we really trying to say here? Does anyone outside this company have any idea what that means?" We human beings (in my mind preferable to just calling ourselves "humans," since that's what machines will one day call us) have a terrible propensity for overcomplicating our communication, and jargon is a big contributor.

ACRONYM MADNESS

There's no shortage of people who argue that jargon within an organization promotes communication efficiency, that it's a verbal shorthand everyone understands. That may be true with acronyms that are specific to a particular company. But too often those within that organization blithely use those same acronyms when speaking externally, to those outside the organization. You know, the KOIs, the ROIs, and the KPIs all make me QPI (question people's intelligence). I encounter this assumption of knowledge frequently, and as a quasi-outsider, I'm constantly stopping conversations to ask what the acronym stands for. The lone exceptions are acronyms that are original and are meant to remind others of a key strategy to embrace, like the famous KISS (keep it simple stupid) or one of our own you'll be hearing in Chapter 12 that alludes to an important mindset in designing your presentation slides: the SAVE principle (sparse and visually engaging). It's important to have these original acronyms spell out a real word, which makes them more memorable. Another one frequently used is SMART: specific, measurable, achievable, relevant, time-bound. Jeff Bezos, the founder of Amazon, revealed one of his favorites to me recently during a coaching session: NATO. No, not the North Atlantic Treaty Organization. His stands for "not attached to any outcome," meaning that sometimes you do something for the benefit of the process without getting hung up on a particular end result. Of all the clients I've worked with over the years, it may not surprise you to learn that the organization most guilty of overdosing on acronyms is the United Nations, the same one that is frequently criticized for allowing its bloated bureaucracy to slow its progress to a crawl. It never ceases to amaze me how direct a correlation there is between the overall efficiency of a particular company or organization and the effectiveness in how they communicate. You show me a company laden with obscure acronyms and jargon and I'll show you a company that is likely light on creativity and originality, and just plain slow.

How ingrained is this artificial language into the psyche of your typical businessperson? Through our survey, we probed to determine how often it occurs. Fewer than one in ten said they "never" use jargon, with the majority admitting that they succumb to it "sometimes."

HOW OFTEN DO YOU LEAN ON JARGON AND CLICHÉ EXPRESSIONS?

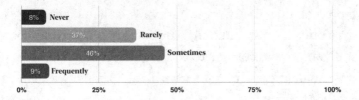

With a scourge as prevalent as jargon, it's only logical that there would be multiple reasons why people eschew simple, straightforward communication. Nearly 40 percent cited either peer pressure ("because everybody else does") or fear of judgment from their peers ("I worry that if I don't use it, people will think I'm less knowledgeable"). Nearly one in three respondents said they view jargon as a totally acceptable style of work communication.

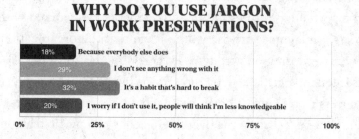

WHY DO YOU USE JARGON IN WORK PRESENTATIONS?

18%	Because everybody else does	
29%	I don't see anything wrong with it	
32%	It's a habit that's hard to break	
20%	I worry if I don't use it, people will think I'm less knowledgeable	

0%   25%   50%   75%   100%

ORIGINALITY = DISTINCTIVENESS

Every opportunity we have to speak publicly is an opportunity to distinguish ourselves from the pack. Before every speech or presentation, the questions we need to ask are, "How can I ensure that I don't sound like everybody else? What can I do that will make the audience say, 'Wow, I've never heard that point made quite that way before!'?" I try to remember Eleanor Roosevelt's quote about the importance of doing something every day that makes you uncomfortable and apply that to giving a presentation. Every presentation, you should challenge yourself to stray outside your traditional comfort zone, even if it's for a few seconds. If you grow accustomed to doing that more and more, you'll feel more confident presenting in a fresh and original way. I'm particularly aware of this when I'm presenting at a company I work with regularly and someone in the room has seen my presentation before. Short of reinventing the wheel and changing the entire deck, I try to include two or three new slides that either address the specific needs of that client or reference something topical and timely that makes clear to the audience the current nature of the content. Short of that, find a different sounding way to articulate a thought they've heard before. When I hear the person who's been in the room before say, "There's stuff in there I don't think I've heard before," then I know I've done my job. Don't ever let them think you're a predictable one-trick pony. That's key to being memorable.

GREATEST-HITS LIST

Day in and day out I come across some real head-scratching examples of jargon, but recently I heard one that actually changed the entire meaning of the sentence. A communications executive, of all people, was telling me that their CEO needed to speak with a higher degree of certainty in his voice. "He has to be more convicted," he said. It was a rather unfortunate jargon-driven choice of words considering that a previous CEO had been accused of improper relationships with female employees. "You mean he needs to speak with more conviction, right?" I asked. "Let's make sure that the word 'convicted' is never coming out of our mouths." That incident reminded me of a word executives in the retail fashion industry love to use to describe the composition and quality of the materials and fabrics: "fabrications." In most social circles, "fabrication" is a diplomatic word used to describe a lie. In the spirits industry, when they speak about the product they make that's inside the bottle, they almost always refer to it as "the liquid." For me, that word conjures up images of a beaker full of undrinkable "liquid" sitting atop a Bunsen burner in eighth-grade chemistry class with a skull-and-bones etched into the glass. I don't know about you, but that's not something I have any interest in pouring over the rocks.

At the time of this writing, there are some examples of jargon that are in vogue. Right now, the jargon flavor of the month is "intentionality." What's wrong with "intent"? Adding four more syllables to a perfectly good word doesn't bring more clarity or make you sound smarter. In fact, you can call it "subtraction by addition." The first cousin of "intentionality" is "choiceful," another one of my pet peeves. "Thoughtful," "selective," and "discerning" have performed admirably in that context for many years and have done nothing to deserve being put out to pasture in favor of a bogus word like "choiceful."

Former White House press secretary Jen Psaki knows a thing or two about communicating in a way that doesn't leave anybody behind. To her, the simplicity of our communication needs to pass a certain test. "I often call it the Mother-in-Law Test. Basically, is the person speaking in accessible language that smart and engaged people who are not experts on the topic would understand? Always avoid overused clichés and make sure it is simple and relatable. The best are connected to what your audience may be experiencing on a day-to-day basis."

Another winner? "Moderninity." I suspect "modern" would suffice in most situations. You may be shaking your head right now, suspicious that I'm making up these stories just for dramatic effect. I wish I was. When I hear people utter nonsensical words like these, I have to summon every ounce of diplomacy to break the hard truth to them gently. At a social media company one time, I was training a top product engineer who told me that he and his team were planning to "conversate" about what to include in an upcoming product launch announcement.

"You mean you're going to talk about it," I said, half-asking, half-correcting him. "Well, yeah," he somewhat sheepishly admitted. I debated moving on from this lesson in being real, but I just couldn't let it drop. "Why don't you just say that then? Why do you have to make up a new word? If you wrote that word on your computer there would be a little red line underneath it signifying that it's not a word that's recognized in the dictionary. And, if it's not in the dictionary, it shouldn't be in your vocabulary."

As you can see, I'm not even railing against the classic jargony terms, like "leverage," or "bandwidth," or "synergy." That battle has been waged and lost. Those words have insinuated themselves into everyday business conversations to such an extent that they have metastasized extensively throughout corporate narratives. "Against" means "for," as in "We're going to leverage these assets *against* our strategy." Tell me how on earth that makes sense. Words like "disintermediate" and "bifurcated" pop up way more than they should. "Upskilling," "level-setting," and "democrative" are some of the new kids on the block that should be run out of town. "Evangelize" is still around, but its first cousin "valorize" just emerged this year. Technically it is in the dictionary, but not in the distorted way it's being used.

When Jay Carney was the White House press secretary during the Obama administration, his job was to make sure he spoke in a way that all Americans would understand. Resisting the temptation to "use a five-dollar word when a fifty-cent word will do," as Mark Twain once said, was essential in communicating clearly and memorably. Carney said, "To win your audience over, you have to use your own voice. And if it's filled with big words you wouldn't use when you're speaking normally, you're going to lose people. Even if the subject is dry, and of course, in a lot of corporate environments, the subject may be dry, you need to make it less so by speaking plainly."

Back in the day, before she hosted a show every weeknight on MSNBC, Stephanie Ruhle was a managing director at Deutsche Bank. As one of the "women of Wall Street," she undoubtedly used a lot of finance-industry jargon just to assimilate into a predominantly male world. But as she was attempting the tricky transition from banker to TV news star, Stephanie knew that she had to jettison the jargon. She understood that her audience was no longer colleagues or clients in the know, but an external audience of middle America. I asked her if one of the reasons presenters lose an audience is that they suffer from the curse of knowledge. Upon hearing the question, she pounced at the opportunity to reply. "I'm going to tell you exactly why. Because they speak like overly educated, learned douchebags. So, as an audience member, when someone is overly articulate and has too fancy vocabulary, I don't want to freaking hear it."

LEXICON ENVY

I chalk up this predilection for pretention (Oops, I'm guilty of it too!) in how we communicate to what I call "lexicon envy." For generations, what set doctors, lawyers, and elected officials apart from other professionals was their reliance on specialized vocabularies that successfully excluded others. All that professional jargon they made liberal use of made them seemingly worth the fees they charged and less open to having their authority questioned. The fewer people who truly understand what you do, the fewer skeptics there will be challenging your decisions. Eventually other professionals caught on, realizing that by instituting their own brand of jargon, they could elevate their importance and value as well.

But even the bread-and-butter jargon industries have a finite tolerance for it. A few years ago, a team of researchers analyzed over 20,000 scientific manuscripts to determine how much jargon was typical in the field of science when studies and papers were published. As a scientist, one of the goals of your work is to have others in your field cite it in their papers. Yet the researchers observed "a negative relationship between the number of jargon words and the number of citations, which significantly decreased as the proportion of jargon in the title increased." The takeaway here is pretty clear: if jargon is curtailing the viral nature of your words and your work, then it's also an obstacle to being memorable.

This is a problem Juliana Silva and I encountered in conducting research for this book. The papers published on virtually every study we found had a stifling amount of jargon, so much so that we often had to go back and reread sections two or three times just to make sense of it. At one point we were tempted to offer our editing services to the authors of the studies just to free their work from the shackles of incomprehensible language. The more we read, the more we thought of Simon Sinek, author of *Start with Why*, and his take on the huge upside of being succinct: "Simple ideas are easier to understand. Ideas that are easier to understand are repeated. Ideas that are repeated change the world."

In the business world, where most knowledge is obtained through osmosis, a group of words gets thrown around so much that the practical meaning gets muddled and lost. Years ago we were doing some pro bono communications training with a wonderful group of lawyers who had dedicated themselves to public defender work, representing clients who could not afford an attorney. In my conversations with them, I noticed that all of them used the word "holistic" over and over. "We take a holistic approach to plea bargains," or "We think holistically about providing legal representation to the underrepresented." Finally, after about the tenth time, I stopped one of the lawyers to ask what they meant by "holistic." "None of us is really sure," she said. "We're just encouraged to say that a lot in our messaging."

"Holistic" has plenty of company: "content," "platform," "democratization," and of course, "ecosystem." Anything today that involves more than one partnership is automatically called an "ecosystem." This word has utterly exhausted me. Every time I hear it, I want to scream because it has been so hopelessly overused. I know people like it because it sounds very environmentally sound and represents a natural way to preserve ecological balance. I get that. But what's being overlooked is the scientific reality that this balance is maintained because certain species prey on others, probably not the predator-prey image that companies want to be promoting.

I freely admit that this list of culprits in the jargon scourge is nowhere near complete. To do that, I would need a book solely dedicated to that phenomenon, and who the heck wants to read that? Every time I make a blog post on the detrimental effects of jargon, I get scores of comments from people who have their own addition to the jargon hit parade. But if only individual words were the problem, we would exist in a world where communication wasn't so obscure and unapproachable. The first cousins of jargon that make the problem worse are the clichéd expressions that have been rendered threadbare from overuse.

FORGETTABLE PHRASES

In our coaching sessions, we display what you could call "the dirty dozen," twelve clichéd phrases in the business world that desperately need their status switched from ubiquitous to extinct. When we put them on the screen, invariably they draw laughter from the clients, followed by the sheepish admission, "Yep! I say just about all of these, all the time." Then I'm usually asked, "What would you say instead of these? Do you have alternative ways of making these points?" Short of making up a couple on the fly (I know, I know, I implored you to avoid spontaneity), I've never had a swap-out list . . . until now.

You want a clue into what is a guaranteed scripted and rehearsed, say-nothing line, that despite its mediocrity has been the darling of the business community for many years? For private tech firms, it's the typical response to the question "When are you planning to go IPO?" For established public companies looking to grow through acquisition, it's often how they handle the M&A question: "How likely are you to acquire another company in your sector?" The dusty, tired, and predictable reply is, "You know, we're just really focused on building a great company." Whenever you hear someone say, "We're just really focused on . . .," you can bet the bank they have been coached to say that by their PR firm, or some colleague who has gone through some paint-by-numbers coaching in the past and is passing along this strategy that has long outlived its shelf life. The only way to make that line worse is to say you're "laser-focused," a universal embellishment that has the opposite effect from its intention in that it immediately makes me question a company's focus.

THE CLICHÉ SWAP-OUT

Instead of saying something everyone else says, it would be better to describe the type of extensive resources, time, and attention being devoted to whatever it is that you're supposedly laser-focused on. The specifics offered in showing instead of telling is what helps make it memorable.

Companies interested in proving how responsive they are to their customers have developed a handful of expressions that migrated into the cliché category faster than normal because people kept leaning into them so heavily. Several big ones come to mind:

- "We put consumers at the heart of everything we do."

  That's certainly a lovely-sounding sentiment, but if you're a food company that knowingly allows harmful ingredients in your products or packaging, then that line could make it sound like you're intentionally trying to compromise the health of your customers.

  The Cliché Swap-Out: "Every decision we make is filtered through one primary consideration: Will this result in a better experience for the people we serve?"

- "Surprising and delighting consumers."

  While officially not jargon, this has been repeated more than enough times to shove it into the clichéd-expressions category.

  The Cliché Swap-Out: "Going beyond what our customers expect."

- "We're consumer-centric."

  There's no faster way to sound like a fully indoctrinated member of corporate America than to have any word followed by "centric."

  The Cliché Swap-Out: "Making our customers happy *is* our purpose."

- "We meet our consumers wherever and whenever they are."

  This message has been overused to the point of absurdity. It's as if every company got together within the past year and collectively agreed to use this phrase over and over again.

  The Cliché Swap-Out: "We deliver whatever our customers need, whenever that need it."

- "Winning the hearts and minds of consumers."

  This sounds a bit like what a cult leader would say, yet I hear it from benevolent people in the business world all the time. If you look it up in Wikipedia, this is what you find: "Winning hearts and minds is a concept occasionally expressed in the resolution of war, insurgency, and other conflicts, in which one side seeks to prevail by making emotional or intellectual appeals to sway supporters of the other side." I would never advise anyone to use an expression that conjures up an us-versus-them dynamic. The other negative association I make with this phrase is one of Teddy Roosevelt's sauciest quotes: "If you've got them by the b***s, their hearts and minds will follow." Also not the kind of message association you want.

The Cliché Swap-Out: "Earning customers' love and loyalty."

- "On a go-forward basis."

I can't even count how many simpler ways there are to say this.

The Cliché Swap-Out: "From now on."

- "Leveraging core assets."

This is such a classic that Weird Al Yankovic included it in a musical spoof he did on ridiculous jargon.

The Cliché Swap-Out: "Playing to our strengths."

- "Future-proofing the business."

When we talk about "waterproofing" or "shatterproofing," it means those developments can't happen. Remember, if you put a stake in the ground in such an absolute way, you will be called on it if you fall short of your own definition of success.

The Cliché Swap-Out: "Preparing for whatever the future holds."

- "It's early innings."

If sports analogies are predictable and tired, then sports clichés are flat-out exhausted.

The Cliché Swap-Out: "It's too early to tell."

- "Guided by our North Star."

When the person who was into camping or astronomy first came up with this, it was probably a fun metaphor, but as they say, familiarity breeds contempt. Whenever everybody else starts saying it too, it's time to find a fresh metaphor.

The Cliché Swap-Out: "Pursuing our purpose."

I'm saving the best—um, I mean, the *worst*—for last. There is one expression that has risen above all others in its overuse.

- "We're on a journey."

   The word "journey" is abused in several different ways, and most of them have absolutely nothing to do with travel. For example, the spa that expresses their desire to be a part of my "wellness journey." There's no journey happening. I'm just there for a massage. It's the sign at the optometrist that says, "We can help you in your eyeglass-frame-selection journey." I never knew that replacing the glasses I left in a cab could be so exotic. Then there's the company that's trying to transform itself, but it's not happening fast enough. The justification the CEO typically gives for the slow pace is, "Listen, this is a journey we're on." Who knows when in the future the word "journey" will fail to be grandiose enough, but when that happens, I'm sure we'll all be on synonym-selection sojourn. The beauty of getting rid of "journey" is that you don't need to replace it with another word. Just get rid of it!

THE CLARITY CHALLENGE

My intent here is not to go on some endless rant about jargon and cliché because I'm some language purist, although that is a noble pursuit for anyone. I have my own quirks and verbal idiosyncrasies I'm trying to eliminate. It's a constant battle. Some days are better than others. But I harp on these bad public-speaking habits because I have only one goal: to make sure you don't sound like everybody else. When your communication is indistinguishable from that of your colleagues, you forfeit distinctiveness. That's too valuable a quality to squander, because the more you blend in, the less you stand out, and the less memorable you are.

   To emphasize this point in a recent coaching session at one of the streaming media companies, I presented six trainees with what we call the Clarity Challenge. "I will buy dinner," I said, "for anyone who can get through the practice round of their presentation without uttering any of the following three phrases:"

1. "So, I want to talk a little bit about . . ."
2. "So, as we think about . . ."
3. "So, let me walk you through . . ."

I figured that by sharing in advance the explicit nature of my ground rules, I would be footing the bill for at least a couple of people's meals.

My credit card never made it out of my pocket.

Not one person could meet the requirements of the Clarity Challenge. Many would unwittingly utter one or more of the forbidden phrases, and then catch themselves immediately after the infraction, blushing as their hands abruptly covered their mouths.

Why was I being such a nitpicky stickler? Because each one of those expressions makes it nearly impossible for you to stand out from the crowd. There's nothing terribly memorable about someone who communicates exactly like the last person you heard present. The more common your word selection and speaking style, the more forgettable you are.

The minute I start buying more dinners than my budget allows, I will be forced to change the nature of the challenge. Clarity Challenge 2 will require the presenter to get through their deck without once saying the words "perspective" or "standpoint." I know you've heard these words a lot, as in "Now, if you look at our performance from a revenue perspective . . ." or "If we measure our future growth potential from a unit-economics standpoint . . ." Sound familiar? I've yet to come across a solid reason why either of these words needs to be a part of these types of sentences. Instead try "Our revenue is fueling our performance" or "Unit economics plays a major role in how we grow in the future." During one practice run of a presentation, I heard the speaker say the word "perspective" twenty-seven times. I know he wasn't even aware he was doing it, which for his sake was probably a good thing, since it isn't a good look.

THE CLICHÉ GRAND SLAM

For those of you who are fans of professional tennis, you know that completing the Grand Slam means winning the Australian Open, French Open, Wimbledon, and U.S. Open all in the same calendar year. It's a tough feat to pull off, but equally difficult is completing what I call the Cliché Grand Slam. When there's a racquet in your hand, it's the accomplishment that likely guarantees entry into the Tennis Hall of Fame. When there's a microphone in your hand, it's a dubious distinction that could land you in the public speaker's Hall of Shame. What makes the Cliché Grand Slam so difficult is that it consists of four different expressions that all mean the same thing. Usually people gravitate to the one that's their favorite. Hearing all four in the same presentation is a rarity. I'm one of the unlucky ones who's witnessed this cliché cluster in action. Here is a visual representation of the four. See if you can guess them:

HINT
THEY ALL MEAN THE SAME THING

Moving clockwise from the upper left corner, they are "let's drill down," "let's do a deep dive," "let's unpack that," and "let's double click on that." If you repeatedly use one or more of these phrases, you're likely stuck in a "rhetoric rut" from which you should work hard to free yourself.

Most of us are comfortable with conformity. It feels familiar. It feels safe. But a public-speaking comfort zone is also a danger zone. The danger it possesses is that it makes you forgettable.

Now that I've shared all the tricks to help you be memorable, and identified all the traps that can make you forgettable, I want to make sure all that knowledge isn't going to waste because your delivery style is lagging behind the quality of your content. In the next chapter, let's chart a course toward a dynamic delivery. Let's do it together, on one condition: we don't call it a "journey."

SAY THIS	NOT THAT
"Simplify"	"Decomplexify"
"Resilience"	"Resiliency"
"Intent"	"Intentionality"
"Dealing directly"	"Disintermediating"

PART IV

PIPES AND POSES

You can have the greatest content in the world, but if your nonverbal communication skills are lacking, your pearls of wisdom might as well be trapped inside an oyster. The next two chapters will ensure that every part of you, from your hands, to your feet, to your facial expressions, to your vocal cords, is working in unison with your words to captivate your audience.

7

BURYING THE ZOMBIE DRONE

*"Your delivery is a little dead, even by corporate
zombie-talk standards."*

One of the many joys of having a ten-year-old living under the same roof is the opportunity to rediscover Charlie Brown cartoons. As a child, I loved the contrast between that eternal optimism that is one of the hallmarks of youthful innocence and the wise-beyond-their-years jaded cynicism that gives *Peanuts* its edginess. Adults almost never make an appearance, but you do occasionally hear them, in a voice that has been described as a trombone murmur. All grown-up dialogue is passed through a "wah wah machine," turning it into an indistinguishable drone. When Charlie Brown's teacher, Mrs. Hagemeyer, does it, it's funny. When we do it in a conference room in front of work colleagues, laughter is likely to give way to snoring.

RUN-ON TALKING

In communication, the two words everyone should be fearful of utter-ing are "and so." That's because presenters fall into this trap where they feel obliged to connect and weave every thought, every sentence into the next. "And so" is the most common of all connectors. It is the verbal comma, frequently placed where a period should be. So, instead of hav-ing attention-grabbing, short, choppy, simple sentences, what comes out of the mouth is the audible equivalent of a run-on sentence. We all know what happens when we read a run-on sentence in print. We lose focus in the middle, stop, and go back to reread the sentence from the beginning in hopes of better following the narrative. That's a perfectly legitimate course of action when you're reading, but it's not an option when you're listening. Your audience doesn't have the luxury of going back and relistening to what you just said. It's gone, for good.

That's particularly frustrating for today's audiences, because in ev-ery other aspect of our lives, we have the ability to rewind and replay something we didn't understand the first time we heard it. Worse yet, if your listeners fail to properly hear or process something you say, their brain is going to momentarily stop and try to figure out the meaning. In the time it takes them to do that, they've now missed your next sentence, which sets in motion this never-ending game of listener lag.

PERIODS VS. COMMAS

Recently on a conference call for a mayoral candidate I've been working with, the campaign manager said that the message was not resonating for one main reason: the candidate spoke in paragraphs. One look at his narrative told the whole story. It had what I call "period deficiency," a lack of that all-important punctuation mark that keeps you from dron-ing on and on. Instead, we have fallen in love with the comma, the peri-od's evil first cousin that demands no verbal restraint on our part. The comma unabashedly invites us to overindulge in introductory clauses and parenthetical phrases. But if you want to captivate an audience and have them hang on your every word, don't show off your flawless sentence syntax and finely crafted prose. That's likely to trigger a snooze-fest. Think of your speaking voice as a violin. Extensive, flowing prose is the equivalent of long, fluid strokes of the bow. In presenting, you should occasionally have the long bow stroke, but it needs to be mixed with a plucking of the strings with your fingers, or what musicians call "pizzicato," which creates short, abrupt notes. These intentional stops and starts are referred to as "thought groups" by those who study language. Each staccato sentence represents an individual thought that is followed by a pause.

This is backed up by a study published in *PLOS One* by communication researchers and academics Yoonji Kim, John J. Sidtis, and Diana Van Lancker Sidtis, all of whom are affiliated with New York University. They concluded that the powerful impact of these thought groups is often overlooked in the workplace. In their findings, it is the collection of many short phrases that creates an optimal vocal pattern for purposeful speech and for having your ideas connect and resonate. The brief silent spaces between and among these thought groups give the audience time to process the information you are communicating and to react emotionally. A run-on, punctuation-free, paragraph-long thought washes over your listener and denies them the opportunity to chew and digest what you're saying before the next massive helping is shoved at them.

When this information inundation of your audience occurs, your listener often feels as though they are constantly playing comprehension catch-up. This can make them feel frustrated and ultimately fatigued.

A team of data scientists from the organization Quantified Communications analyzed more than 100,000 presentations from corporate executives, politicians, and keynote speakers. They found that effective communicators' messages tend to be more concise than those from speakers who were rated as average or below average. Many presenters speak the way they write, using complex sentences with introductory clauses and parenthetical phrases. This works well in writing, but when you're presenting, it's hard to deliver content that is created that way. It's also confusing for your audience to follow. We discussed some effective strategies for creating content for the ear, rather than the eye, in Chapter 2.

THE CRYSTAL BUTTON

One effective strategy for keeping your audience in lockstep with you is what I call the "crystal button." Here's how it works. If you feel you have droned on too long with a run-on explanation (we're all susceptible to it) that is littered with disjointed tangents, immediately follow it up with a superconcise and punchy crystallizing of what you just said that uses different words. This is typically what we call "buttoning your thought." Here's an example, one that I hope never comes close to crossing your lips: "As we endeavor to optimize synergies and streamline our operational framework, it's imperative that we proactively engage in cross-functional collaborations to leverage best practices and drive sustainable growth, and so, through strategic alignment and agile methodologies, we aim to enhance stakeholder value and capitalize on emerging market opportunities, thereby solidifying our position as market leaders."

With communication like that around, who needs Ambien?

Let's say you inadvertently caught yourself slipping into old, bad habits, uttering this word-salad nonsense. You can partially redeem yourself by immediately following it with this crystal button:

"In other words . . . greater efficiency requires more collaboration if we want to continue growing and leading the market."

Take a long, hard look at either your scripted remarks or, if you have access to it, the transcript of what you said. Then be your own brutal editor. Make it a game to see how synthesized you can get your more granular points. Your audience will thank you.

Our communication style should never create hard work for our listeners. Every time I am in an audience and the presenter makes listening to them an arduous chore, I find myself feeling not just fatigued, but annoyed. When a presenter is opaque and forgettable, the audience leaves feeling as though they've wasted their precious time. They leave with nothing learned, no insights gained, nothing actionable imparted, and nothing memorable to keep. Every time you plan a presentation, imagine you're hosting a party and ask yourself, "What's in the idea goodie bag everyone leaves with?" What's the one piece of wisdom I'm going to generously gift to those who invested their valuable time in listening to me? If they leave empty-handed, your reputation takes a hit in what is seen as a missed opportunity.

THE TEN-MINUTE WARNING

Cognitive scientists have a reasonably good idea of when audiences stop listening to a presentation. It occurs at the ten-minute mark. According to molecular biologist John Medina, people seem to get bored after approximately ten minutes—and it occurs in a class lecture or a business presentation.

It's safe to assume that your content requires more than ten minutes to deliver. Fortunately, there are several easy-to-implement tips that will reengage your audience and hold their attention.

The common theme that connects each of the following five tips is *change.* Neuroscientists have found that the best way to reengage a person's attention when it begins to wane is to change up the format of the content.

THE VOICE

Usually the idea of achieving consistency is a desired goal, but not when it comes to our voices. The less we vary the sound of them, the less engaged the listener.

That was the conclusion reached in a study out of Stanford University's Graduate School of Business. The research found that even just a 10 percent increase in vocal variety can have a highly significant impact on your audience's attention to and retention of your message.

A study of the most popular TED Talks also points to variety as an essential element in memorable communication. The most successful speakers have a 30.5 percent higher vocal variety than other, less popular speakers.

In addition to the length and structure of our thoughts, we also want to bring variation to our vocal velocity, vibe, and volume. How's that for alliteration?

VELOCITY

In my experience as a coach, the earlier people are in their career, the more likely they are to speak too fast. A lack of confidence standing in front of the room triggers a flight response that makes sitting back down in your seat as quickly as possible the number one priority, the let's-just-get-this-over-with mentality.

Research conducted by the National Alliance on Mental Illness (NAMI) found that anxiety disorders can affect the way people speak, leading to speech that is faster. They found that anxiety is a common cause of racing through thoughts and speaking faster, both of which can make communication more difficult. People who are anxious may feel like they can't keep up with their thoughts and may speak much faster as a result, which can cause stuttering or slurring.

Your speaking velocity—or as Major League Baseball players today call it, "velo"—tells your audience a lot about you. If you go too fast, the likelihood is that they will see you as nervous, insecure, or inexperienced.

Flying through your speech or presentation strips you of your ability to project command and gravitas. It also sets you up to make more mistakes and stumbles. The key concept here is "mastery before speed." The better you know your content, the more you can gradually and incrementally increase your velo. Think back to our earlier analogy of you're driving in your car and suddenly you see a big pothole in the road. If you're driving fast, there's no time to swerve around it. But if your speed is more moderate and under control, you have sufficient time to react, adjust, and avoid driving into it. Of course, if you've driven that road multiple times, you can accelerate with more confidence because you know where that pothole is.

In the middle of a presentation, that mental pothole that materializes without warning could be uncertainty over what point you want to make next or a problem with word retrieval. Anyone who has ever spoken to an audience knows it is rarely smooth sailing from start to finish. We're all susceptible, even if we're well prepared, to hit a bumpy stretch. When this happens, it's imperative that you slow down. This will give your brain sufficient time to navigate far ahead of your mouth and selectively choose what conversational road you're going to take and what words you'll use to articulate that thought. Under normal circumstances, our brains are 600 milliseconds ahead of our mouths. By adding even a brief pause, we can dramatically increase the amount of time available for us to contemplate our next verbal move.

We asked the respondents in our survey (see below) to look inward and analyze why they speak too fast in their work settings. Overwhelmingly, the top reason was nerves, with just under half blaming jitters for their breakneck speed. But about 35 percent cited reasons tied to their belief that they will be rewarded instead of punished by an audience for breaking the speed limit.

WHAT'S THE BIGGEST REASON YOU SPEAK TOO FAST PRESENTING TO OTHERS?

48%	I get nervous
21%	I think speaking fast makes me look smarter
14%	I worry that slowing down will make me look less energetic
17%	I just want to get through it

0%   25%   50%   75%   100%

But these are not the only reasons why we speak too fast. A lack of brevity in our prepared remarks or presentation is also a culprit. I work with many people who struggle to streamline their presentations and fall victim to the misguided notion that they need to include absolutely everything, for fear they will leave some question unanswered. That's what I call the "kitchen sink syndrome," which often makes people try to jam twenty minutes of content into a fifteen-minute window. In your mind, you're thinking, "Wow, I've got a lot to cover in this deck, I'd better get through it quickly." When that thought is gnawing away in the back of your mind, it's very difficult to assume a relaxed, controlled pace. You would be much better off taking a machete to your content and start slashing away. Aim instead for twelve to thirteen minutes or less of content so you can let it breathe, take your time with it, and take the pressure off yourself.

Using less than your allotted speaking time is also a great way to boost your popularity among your colleagues. Who doesn't love somebody who gets right to it, doesn't drone on, and employs an economy of words to say what needs to be said? It's the rare meeting or event that sticks to the schedule, so if you use only twelve of your fifteen minutes, you're contributing mightily to getting things back on track. I know that anyone who helps me depart a meeting quicker becomes my new personal hero. Conversely, those who take three minutes to communicate what only needed forty seconds find their way onto my Ten Most Unwanted List.

The speakers who take their time, and benefit from the underutilized technique of pausing, not only commit fewer errors but also give the impression that they are savoring the opportunity to connect and communicate. This allows the speaker to come across as more calm, confident, and experienced. The ideal range is between 145 and 170 words per minute. Google Play has a Speech Rate Meter that can help you calculate your pace. Mastering the proper speaking "velo" can boost your executive presence.

VIBE

According to body language researcher and UCLA psychology professor Albert Mehrabian, your tone of voice accounts for 38 percent of the impact you make when sharing your feelings or attitudes. I often say to the people we train, "If you were presenting to me in a foreign language I did not understand, I would still want to be able to determine whether you were saying something positive or negative, just from the pitch and intonation of your voice."

Not Lost in Translation

Interestingly, a study by M. D. Pell and others published in 2009 revealed that monolingual Spanish speakers were able to accurately identify the emotion in a speaker's voice even in languages they did not understand: English, German, and Arabic. They were able to accurately gauge whether the speaker was angry, sad, bored, fearful, or happy.

There's no better way to inspire or motivate people with your words than to be memorable, especially given that the actions people take at your urging are often carried out hours, days, or even weeks later. For people to follow through, you must be memorable because the data on retaining spoken information are working against you.

Studies indicate that immediately following the presentation, the audience remembers 50 percent of what was said. By the next day, the audience remembers 25 percent. A week later, it's just 10 percent.

That means that even more important than what you say is how you say it, the vibe you're giving off when you speak. Frequently this is what is called tone of voice or intonation, and it carries enormous power in how we interpret the information we share with others.

In a 2011 study published in the *Swiss Journal of Psychology*, authors Hede Helfrich and Philipp Weidenbecher set out to better understand the effect of vocal pitch on attention and memory. They found that retention of content in long-term memory was higher when individuals listened to voices using high and low voice pitches, as opposed to a medium voice pitch. This finding was consistent regardless of whether the individuals listened to natural voices or voices that had been digitally manipulated to affect intonation. So this may be one of those rare cases where playing consistently straight down the middle can work against you.

Same Words, Different Meaning

Recently I asked the manager of a store where I frequently shop how one of his new employees was working out. "He's good," he said. Seeing that in print, without hearing how it was said, doesn't tell you the whole story. Had it been said in a firm, consistent pitch, it would have been clear that he had made a great hire. But the delivery had an undulation of pitch signaling a lukewarm endorsement, the kind you might give when telling a friend that the movie you saw was "just okay." Bottom line? The manager's tone told me he was having second thoughts about his new employee, even though his words indicated something different. This is supported by research by ScienceDirect concluding that intonation is how we express emotion. It adds meaning to the content of a message that is not already expressed in the semantics of its individual words.

How we say things is frequently underestimated in the crucial role it plays in creating nuances of meaning, how it reveals our emotional reactions, and how it heightens or hinders our executive presence—that quality we keenly look for in our leaders that fosters an air of confidence and the ability to persuade and influence. Manipulation of our intonation spares us from the need to repeatedly hammer a point into the ground, because studies show that emotionally expressed information is retained in memory following just a single exposure.

These findings support the hypothesis that emotional information achieves prominence and leaves traces in our mind. As a result, they are more likely to be converted into long-term memory.

I'm often struck at how often presenters get stuck in a monotone groove when they are trying to persuade or influence their audience. To motivate or inspire your audience to take action, your voice needs to rise to reflect the optimism you feel for how positive the outcome is likely to be if your suggestion or strategy is followed. You are creating the awareness that you have visualized the end result, that you have seen over to the other side of the mountain and are energized by the enormous possibilities and opportunities that lie ahead. Very simply, those words will fall flat if your voice is flat. Research shows that higher vocal pitch is associated with joy, anticipation, and eagerness, whereas a deeper tone underscores sadness and calmness.

I find that exceptional public speakers pay a great deal of attention to the pitch of their voice. They are keenly aware and very intentional in manipulating their tone to convey the proper emotion, yet in our survey, only about 20 percent said they do it frequently, while the number of people who said they never do it, or rarely do it, was about 30 percent.

HOW OFTEN DO YOU CONSCIOUSLY MANIPULATE THE TONE OF YOUR VOICE TO EMPHASIZE AN EMOTION OR ATTITUDE?

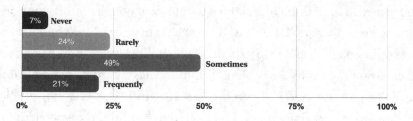

The intonation of our voice also has an enormous impact on our perceived executive presence. One of the common vocal traits I notice in my work is what we call "uptalk," the rise in pitch at the end of a sentence that makes the thought sound more like a question than a statement. I've heard some describe it as "Valley Girl Syndrome," which is a gross misnomer given that the scourge has migrated and spread far from what's believed to be its original source. It's not unlike the destructive East Asian "Frankenfish" that was discovered in Lake Michigan in 2004. That freshwater predator decimated entire ecosystems.

Uptalk possesses an equal power of potential destruction as it contin-
ues unabated in contaminating the style of communication throughout
corporate America.

Another school of thought has uptalk originating in Australia, where
it is so prominent, it's been assigned its own acronym: AQI, or Australian Question Intonation. But regardless of where it originated, if you
take uptalk, and throw in some "vocal burn" for good measure (think
of the intolerably gravelly sound of RFK Jr. reserved for the end of a
sentence), then you have an audio experience that's more than a bit
tough on the ears.

Uptalk has also been called a "sexy baby vocal virus" by actor, writer,
and director Lake Bell in her 2013 movie, *In a World*. The impetus for
making the film, according to Bell, was to address a vocal trait that
studies indicate keeps women from advancing in their careers and from
being taken seriously.

Uptalk as a career impediment is only logical, given that the vocal
pitch associated with uptalk mimics that of a question. Posing a question instead of making a declarative statement compromises your perceived conviction and gravitas. But societal pressures on women to be
less opinionated could help explain why uptalk exists. This is part of the
conclusion drawn by Robin Lakoff in the study "Language and Woman's Place," published in *Language in Society* in 1973: "The marginality
and powerlessness of women is reflected in both the ways women are
expected to speak, and the ways in which women are spoken of. In
appropriate women's speech, strong expression of feeling is avoided,
expression of uncertainty is favored."

This could likely be a factor in why prefacing a statement with "I
think" or "I believe" tends to be a habit among women more than men.
As a speech coach who, on average, works with more women than
men, I am on a crusade to inspire women to equivocate less.

In a 2021 study conducted for *Social Psychology* titled "The Voice
Gives It Away: Male and Female Pitch as a Cue for Gender Stereotyp-
ing," the role of vocal pitch was examined as it pertains to perceived au-

thority. Participants listened to a text read by a female speaker, whose voice pitch was manipulated to be high or low. The finding? The high-pitched female speaker was rated as less competent.

The findings of studies like that, or perhaps just the societal awareness of vocal bias, could have been a primary reason why Elizabeth Holmes artificially altered the pitch of her voice. Holmes, as you may recall, is the disgraced founder and CEO of Theranos, a company that she claimed could perform an array of medical tests from just a few drops of blood. Holmes became a Silicon Valley darling almost overnight, with Theranos achieving a $9 billion valuation (her worth was estimated at $5 billion) just a few years after she started it at age nineteen. All the elements of a great media story were in place, and Holmes did her job in milking them for all they were worth.

She worked to project a "female Steve Jobs" image, wearing similar black mock turtlenecks and even naming one of her products "the 4s" after the iPhone model. She poached some of Apple's designers to work on the look and feel of one of her products. She seemed to be the antithesis of the typical tech CEO, but she wanted to make sure she didn't differ from her peers in every department. Employees at Theranos claimed that Holmes used a fake deep voice to project more executive presence, a claim Holmes did not deny. In a 2023 *New York Times* profile, Holmes admitted that she had created a "character" in order to be "taken seriously and not taken as a little girl, or a girl who didn't have good technical ideas." She added, "Maybe people picked up on that not being authentic, since it wasn't."

Holmes is not the first high-profile woman to change the intonation of her voice to bolster her perceived gravitas. Margaret Thatcher, who was Britain's prime minister from 1979 to 1990, had a much higher voice early in her political career and was concerned that she would never make it to 10 Downing Street unless that changed. She had heard an actor named Barrie Ingham on the radio, voicing over commercials for the Conservative Party. She was impressed with Ingham's ability to command the listener's attention just by controlling the pitch of his voice. It was a skill that was essential in his work as a Royal Shakespearean actor and one that he would personally teach to Thatcher in her assent to leadership. It's hard to imagine that Russian president Mikhail Gorbachev would have dubbed Thatcher "The Iron Lady" if she had had a high, squeaky voice.

In the political arena here in the United States, vocal pitch may be the surest indicator of a winning candidate. Studies show that politicians with more attractive voices are perceived more positively than politicians with less attractive voices. Furthermore, social psychologists in 2002 analyzed audiotapes from nineteen U.S. presidential debates between 1960 and 2000 and found that those candidates who had more acoustic energy concentrated at lower vocal frequencies won the popular vote in *all* eight elections they looked at.

You could have the most dynamic sound to your voice, one that is fluctuating effectively in both the lower and higher ends of the register, and your message can still lay there as limp as a strand of overcooked pasta if your word choice is bland and fails to evoke a powerful emotional response. Experiments conducted on word recognition show that experiences associated with high emotional arousal are better remembered than experiences with low emotional arousal. So taking that all-business, just-the-facts-ma'am approach is a surefire way to be forgotten. More specifically, their research yielded a linear relationship between level of emotional arousal and long-term memory. The higher the intensity of emotional arousal caused at the time of communicating, the higher the long-term recognition scores.

VOLUME

Anyone who has ever taught young students has learned the hard way the futility of shouting. Logically, it seems like a booming voice would be the best way to bulldoze your way to engagement and retention. It doesn't work that way. Often, the higher your decibel level, the greater degree of tune-out you'll get. It can be hard to embrace this tactic given how utterly counterintuitive it is. But the truly great speakers are the ones who identify their punch line, the takeaway thought meant to stick, and consciously dial back their projection to make the audience lean in further to hear the payoff. The trick here is not to trail off in intensity at the end of the thought, but rather to ratchet up the sense of urgency and enthusiasm behind the thought to balance the lower volume.

A textbook example of this is a video from *Fortune*'s Most Powerful Women Summit in 2017. Mellody Hobson, the CEO and cofounder of Ariel Investments, launched into a story about a quandary a fellow CEO found himself in:

"[He] had an open position for comms in his organization and he had no people of color in the executive ranks. So he went to the executive recruiter and he said, 'I want a diverse slate.' The executive recruiter came back and said he couldn't find anyone. So, he went back to the executive team and said, 'Got it. We couldn't find anyone, so we're not going to fill the position. So, we're not going to have a head of comms inside this publicly traded company.' The general counsel, the CFO panic! Like we can't run a public company without a head of communications. Suddenly, there was a diverse slate."

Classic Storytelling Structure

The story is masterfully executed in terms of both structure and delivery. She **sets the scene** succinctly: this company has an open position for comms and they want a diverse candidate to be strongly considered. Then she **establishes the tension**: the executive recruiter informs the CEO that he couldn't find diverse candidates, which prompts the CEO to hold off on filling the position. Then comes the **resolution/outcome**: under the threat of leaving the position vacant, suddenly a diverse slate appears. Hobson is well aware of her punch line, "Suddenly, there was a diverse slate," which she delivers in a lower-volume voice. The sentence immediately before that, which captures the height of the tension in the story, is delivered in a full-throated, passionate way, which makes the dramatic drop-off in projection for the punch line that follows even more dramatic.

For example, several experiments conducted at the National Library of Medicine, which is part of the National Institutes of Health, have demonstrated that confident speakers tend to intentionally communicate at an objectively louder volume relative to unconfident speakers. Early research on vocal perception illustrated the relationship between vocal loudness and perceived confidence by instructing speakers to read a passage using either a confident or unconfident voice. The results indicated that speakers instructed to speak in a confident voice naturally spoke louder. They also found that speakers who were asked to communicate in a confident manner not only spoke at a louder volume, but were also perceived as more confident by listeners.

SILENCE IS GOLDEN

If you're successful in speaking in shorter, choppier sentences and slowing down, there is one potential downside you need to keep front of mind: the barbarians of filler words waiting outside the gate. But nearly all of us have had that guarded perimeter profoundly penetrated by a well-known marauding gang composed of "so," "um," "like," "kind of," "sort of," and "you know." It's human nature to be uncomfortable with silence. It's known as "sedatephobia."

Research conducted in the Netherlands found that it takes only four seconds of silence in conversation for Americans to feel rattled, rejected, or insecure. That's in stark contrast to the Japanese, who were found in another study to be perfectly comfortable sitting in silence for more than eight seconds.

To avoid that awkwardness, we will fill every crack and crevice of available audio space, for fear that allowing "dead air" will make us seem unfocused and indecisive. But the irony here is that the most confident presenters are the ones who feel totally comfortable letting you watch them be selective in what they say. In the words of the ancient Chinese philosopher Lao Tzu, "Silence is a source of great strength."

Taking enough time to be thoughtful and selective is also a sign of respect to your audience. It means that you're strategizing in real time how to articulate your thoughts in the most concise, accurate, and impactful way. It is unlikely your audience will assume you've lost your place or that you forgot what to say next. That's merely what our undermining inner voices tell us. Anyone can stand in front of a room and start speaking without clear intention, but the likely product of that is a rambling, redundant, and fragmented monologue that will be forgettable and disposable. In fact, research out of Stanford shows that presentations that are carefully structured are retained 40 percent more than ones that are free-form and unstructured.

THE KEY IS VARIATION

Again, it's about living on the edges, and preferably not just one edge but both of them: brisk and slow, high- and low-pitched, a shout and a whisper. This intentional state of variance is what captivates your audience and what makes them remember you more. Now let's make sure that random and distracting gesticulations and body movements don't make you memorable for all the wrong reasons.

DO THIS	NOT THAT
Speak in Short, Choppy Sentences	Connect Thoughts into Complex Sentences
Slow Down over Your Most Important Points	Go Fast at All Times to Bolster Energy
For Dramatic Emphasis, Lower Your Volume	Hit All Your Big Points Louder and Harder
Embrace the Power of Pausing	Keep Your Flow of Sound Constant

8

THE RICKY BOBBY QUANDARY

"I'M NOT SURE WHAT TO DO WITH MY HANDS"

"If you forget to walk the stage, don't worry. I'll cue you by sending a little electrical shock through your wireless microphone."

In Chapter 4, we discussed the value of injecting humor into your communications, a powerful tool you should never pass up an opportunity to wield. Think of it as a tantalizingly effective way of beckoning people into the subject matter of your presentation. My colleagues and I use it all the time, especially when emphasizing points repeatedly. As a presenter, the more you say the same thing over and over again, the more you need to make it fun for yourself, just to keep your own interest level high. This is true when it comes to the number one question clients ask in training sessions: "What do I do with my hands?" We do thoroughly answer the dos and don'ts of hand placement and gesticulation (as I will here shortly), but to pique their interest, we lead that explanation with a clip from the movie *Talladega Nights*, in which Will Ferrell plays a simple-minded racecar driver named Ricky Bobby. In one scene, Ricky is doing a postrace interview for TV, during which his hands are slowly drifting up from his waist to his shoulders, when he suddenly interrupts his answer to say in a hillbilly drawl, "I'm not sure what to do with my hands." In the humor department, it's not exactly my cup of tea, but nearly every client, from everyperson to the top executive, absolutely howls with laughter. Now, in the immediate wake of that feel-good, funny moment, I've got their heightened attention to make the instruction on effective body language resonate deeper. So now you know the meaning behind the name of this chapter, although proper hand placement and movement is just one aspect of positive body language.

If devoting ample time to crafting a speech or presentation was all that was needed for us to captivate an audience, our public-speaking lives would be infinitely easier. But all indicators point to the supreme importance of our nonverbal communication skills. Remember, an astounding 55 percent of the emotions behind our communication is conveyed through body language, yet that is the aspect of presenting that we often give the least thought to and dedicate zero time to practicing.

To become a well-rounded and accomplished public speaker, fully embrace the reality that presenting to an audience, either in person or virtually, is a performance. Put aside any misguided notion that treating it as such is a cheesy tactic that compromises your professionalism. In fact, what might seem a little over-the-top to you, in terms of projection and animation, is probably just about right. That's why videotaping yourself is such a valuable exercise. Very few of us are capable of accurately assessing the energy and enthusiasm we're injecting into our presentations. Many a presenter who has allowed the fear of seeming too theatrical to hold them back has underperformed in their speaking opportunities with audiences and failed to have their ideas resonate. When we videotape our clients' practice presentations and show the recording back to them, the most common reaction they have is, "Wow, I look kind of bored!" What's often tamping down their energy is a lack of focus on their nonverbal communication skills. How you command the space around you plays a major role in how you're perceived. Here is a checklist of all the factors taken in chronological order. Some of the key considerations need to be addressed a day or two in advance of your talk:

WHAT TO WEAR

I don't profess to have the know-how of a stylist, but there are some basic principles that will help ensure that your wardrobe builds your confidence and doesn't serve as a distraction. Regardless of how styles change, or workwear evolves, ask yourself, "What do I want my clothes to say about who I am? What image am I trying to project: casual, professional, formal?" If you're speaking at an event or to a group of clients, always call in advance and ask about the dress code, then go half a notch more professional. So, if it's described as business casual, don't wear jeans and a short-sleeved polo shirt, even if that's what everyone else will be wearing. You would be better off in an open-neck dress shirt and a sport jacket. I also make wardrobe selections based on the industry in which I'll be working that day. What I wear to a Wall Street law firm differs significantly from what I wear to a tech startup. It's often a delicate balance between fitting in and standing out.

Regardless of industry, setting, or audience composition, there are a few ironclad rules. Your clothes should be free of rips, stains, and wrinkles. Shoes don't need to spotlessly gleam like a marine's, but they also shouldn't look like you slogged through a muddy trail to get there. Also, check the bottoms of your shoes. If they are worn to paper-thin status or have a hole, get them resoled. If you're sitting on a stage for an industry panel or a fireside chat, the audience can see the bottoms of your shoes. If there's a hole there, they may wonder if you hitchhiked to the venue. Looking crisp doesn't mean being dressed up. If it's an important presentation, wear something that makes you feel supremely confident. That little bit of self-assuredness will show up in your body language.

Conversely, anything about your wardrobe or grooming that makes you feel insecure or self-conscious will serve as a distraction and will negatively impact the nonverbal signals you are sending to the audience.

BE AWARE OF YOUR SURROUNDINGS

Surprises are a wonderful thing if you're eight years old and it's your birthday. But they're a terrible thing if something unexpected throws you for a loop minutes before you present to an audience. The confidence and professionalism you project through your body language are directly correlated to how well you anticipated ten factors relating to the physical surroundings and the technology at the venue. In advance, ask:

QUESTION	REASON FOR ASKING
What color scheme is planned for the stage?	If the backdrop is red and black, it's probably not wise to wear a red blouse and a black skirt. If you do, you could end up dissolving into the background.
What microphone will I be using?	If you're going to be using a handheld mic, that's what you want to be practicing with. If you're going to be wearing a headset mic, don't wear big hoop earrings that might clank against the microphone bar.
Is there a podium?	If not, you'll need to practice walking the stage more and not having a place to prop up your laptop or written notes.
Will there be confidence monitors in front of the stage, and if so, how many will there be and where will they be positioned?	There should be at least one monitor showing your slides and one for your script or presenter's notes.
Where's the water?	To avoid having a Marco Rubio moment, always know where onstage you can access a glass or bottle of drinking water. In the midst of a coughing spell onstage is not the time to go searching for it.
Will I be sitting? If so, on what?	If the event is planning on counter-height stools, be aware that hemlines and trouser cuffs tend to hike up higher than you might want.

Will I be advancing my own slides with a clicker?	If you are, put fresh batteries in your clicker and give it a test.
Is someone introducing me? If so, what's their preferred method of handing things off: Handshake? Hug? Fist bump?	You want to make sure the person introducing you doesn't extend their hand for a shake while you go for a hug. Awkward!
Will there be a countdown clock at the foot of the stage?	If so, ask the event organizers if they can make the clock count *up* from zero to show your running time. Watching a clock slowly run out of time, like sand falling in an hourglass, creates more anxiety.
Check the weather forecast.	If you have to present at a location outside your office, make sure that neither rain nor hot, humid weather has you arriving soaking wet. If avoiding the elements isn't possible, wear a white shirt. Gray or blue will clearly show perspiration.

Here's an unexpected piece of advice. If you're speaking at an event large enough to have a full production crew, get the name of the AV technician ahead of time. That way, if anything goes wrong in mid-presentation, let's say with a clicker that's not working, you can calmly say in the crew's direction, "Hey, Kim, do me a favor please? Hand me the spare clicker. For some reason this one decided to stop working." That demonstrates much more stage command and calm than if you were to say, "Um . . . I think we have a problem up here. Can somebody help with this?" Even if everything is imploding around you, never allow even a hint of stress to creep into your voice. I've seen more than my share of presenters come completely unglued over what is a relatively minor snafu. Audiences smell public-speaking panic like sharks smell blood in the water, and given the crucial nature of those first few seconds, don't let them see you sweat before you've gotten into the heart of your presentation.

Several hours before you're scheduled to speak, ask to have access to the exact space in which you'll be presenting. Walk the stage. Get a feel for the room. Speak to the back row to get a sense of how much projection you'll need to be heard. Ask the technical crew to turn on the lights to the brightness level they'll be at for your talk. I've seen many an executive come onstage and squint from the intensity of the stage lights like a suspect being interrogated by the police. Test out the production crew's clicker. It may differ from the one you're used to. You want to make sure the advance button doesn't stick if you press it for more than a second, unwittingly advancing your deck two slides at a time instead of one.

If the teleprompter operator is there, ask them to run through the first five minutes of your script with you. This will help them get a feel for your delivery speed and where you deviate from the script with ad-libbed content. If you're being introduced by the host of the event or the preceding speaker, ask to see their script. This will help you plan in advance a way to riff off their introduction that creates the illusion of spontaneity. This happened to me in Minnesota in 2023 when I was asked to give a presentation to the entire group that reports to the chief technology officer at a major bank. The CTO planned to introduce me after the group came back from lunch, so while everyone was eating, I went into the now-empty auditorium and asked the teleprompter operator to show me the CTO's script. In it, he was going to share a quote from the late auto industry titan Lee Iacocca, who said, "You can have brilliant ideas, but if you can't get them across, your brains won't get you anywhere." Uh-oh! One of the first slides in my deck was a video clip of Warren Buffett saying almost the exact same thing: "One easy way to become fifty percent more than what you are is to hone your communication skills. If you can't communicate, it's like winking at a girl in the dark—nothing happens. So, you can have all the brainpower in the world, but you have to be able to transmit it."

Oh no! Of all the quotes to pull, why did this have to be the one? Time for some quick thinking or else I'll sound like I'm just drafting off the CTO. Rather than delete the Buffett clip, I decided to play it but acknowledge the four-hundred-pound gorilla in the room. So my impromptu plan was to follow the clip by saying, "Looks like Warren

needs to not only update his last-century analogies, but he should probably stop plagiarizing other executives."

All these considerations underscore a basic truth: familiarity breeds
comfort. The more accustomed you are to the specifics of the venue,
and how things are going to unfold, the more at home you will seem
and the less anxious you're likely to feel.

IT'S SHOWTIME!

Okay, so you've done all the advance due diligence. It's time to execute. Let's take this in chronological order. It begins with your walk
out onstage. You look more confident and relaxed if you begin speaking two or three steps before you hit "your mark" onstage, that little
X on the ground made from gaffer's tape showing where you should
stand, at least initially. It doesn't sound like an important consideration, but if you see a speaker hit their stage mark, stop, then begin
speaking after a full beat or two of pause, it looks amateurish and
stilted.

If there's a microphone attached to a podium, adjust it to the right position for your height, *before* you begin speaking. Changing the angle of
the microphone's flexible stem can sound like you're trying to remove
a rusty bolt. There's no sense in fighting to have your opening line be
heard over that awful sound. What's worse is not bothering to adjust
it at all. Years ago, I attended a memorial service for a media executive
who had been my boss. One of the highest-ranking executives from
this global media conglomerate stepped up to the lectern to deliver a
eulogy. This man was at least six foot, three inches tall. The preceding
speaker was about five foot five, a height disparity that was apparently
lost on him, because he never bothered to adjust the microphone up-
ward. I'm sure he prepared an eloquent tribute to his lifelong colleague,
but nobody heard a word he said because the mic was pointed at his tie
clip instead of his mouth.

WHAT DO I DO WITH MY HANDS?

Whenever you do something that looks unintended or awkward, the audience's attention shifts from the message you're delivering to whatever looks strange about your body language. That's why it's so important for everything you do to look fluid and natural. When you're standing in front of a group of your colleagues or a larger audience, looking like you're in command of the situation starts with your hands. The worst thing you can do is demonstrate utter confusion over where to place them. Maybe they start off in front of you in a "fig leaf" position, but then only two seconds later you're raising them to put them in your pockets, but uh-oh, your hands can't quite find your pocket openings, and you don't want to look like you're struggling to do something so simple, so you give up on the pocket idea and put your hands behind your back. A few seconds into that pose you have a moment of introspection and realize that posture is too meek, so you bring your hands back around to the front and fold your arms across your chest. Suddenly your mind flashes back to some article you read a couple of years ago on how folding your arms creates an unwelcoming and closed-off vibe for the audience, so you drop them, and now they're dangling at your sides, another awkward place for them. All this manual meandering has taken place over the course of twenty seconds. Those optics create an impression of uncertainty that signals to the audience that you're battling an acute case of nerves. The survey shows that the majority of respondents may very well contend with this problem, given that they rest their hands in a position that is not ideal.

WHAT'S YOUR FAVORITE RESTING POSITION FOR YOUR HANDS WHEN YOU'RE STANDING FOR A PRESENTATION?

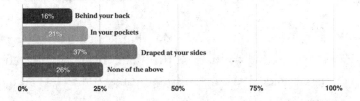

Have your upper arm and your forearm form a right angle so that your hands come together right around your navel. Your hand muscles should be relaxed and soft, as if you're handling something very delicate. The tension you may be experiencing from public-speaking nerves will create a rigidity in your muscles, so be intentional about keeping them relaxed. It's best not to interlock your fingers, clench your hands, or create the shape of a triangle. That was once the position of choice for TV reporters, but we're not in the 1980s anymore, so unless you want to look like a fossil stuck in some time warp, scrap the triangle. Have your palms facing in, almost resting against your torso and the backs of your hands facing out to the audience. This is the information Ricky Bobby was desperate to have as he stood in the winner's circle. From this position, it's easy to move them to punctuate the message you're delivering.

Striking this pose is easier if you're using a clicker. By holding the device with both hands (one hand holding the top and the other holding the bottom), your hands will be anchored right where they should be. A couple of brief words of caution about the clicker. Don't fall victim to what we call the "clicker punch." This is when the speaker extends their arm and punches the air with the clicker in some misguided belief that this motion will make the slides advance more dependably. The irony here is that the presenter often clicker-punches in the direction of the screen they're projecting onto, not in the other direction toward their laptop.

There's no reason to ever take your finger off the clicker button that advances your slides. The act of pressing it is meant to be done inconspicuously. When the presenter looks down at the clicker every time they want to click to advance, they don't look as though they're in command.

If you don't have a clicker, take the thumb and forefinger of your right hand, gently hold the nail on the index finger of your left hand. Now you're in the ideal resting position. At first it may feel odd, maybe even uncomfortable, but people get used to this position quickly. I guarantee that from now on, you'll notice professional presenters keeping their hands in exactly this position.

HOW DO I MOVE MY HANDS?

Many times when I ask clients what they would like to work on to change their style of presenting or their delivery, their answer is, "Well, I talk a lot with my hands, so that's a big problem." To that I reply, "And the problem with that is?" I find that this aspect of public speaking carries with it more misconceptions than almost any other, erroneous beliefs that talking with your hands is something to suppress. I've been told this was the guidance given by a previous speech coach. When I hear that, my first order of business is to undo the damage done by that bad advice. Our survey clearly points to an overall reluctance to use hand movement while speaking, with less than 30 percent saying they use their hands frequently and with a sense of purpose. That's less than the number of people who said they never do it because they've been advised not to plus those who do it rarely.

DO YOU GESTICULATE WITH YOUR HANDS WHEN YOU PRESENT?

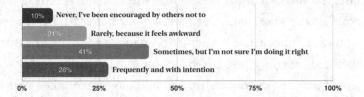

If your hands seem to have a mind of their own, don't brainwash them into doing anything too rehearsed or choreographed. Let your hands do what they want to do, as long as you stay away from four particular movements:

1. **The Metronome:** This happens when your hands make any repetitive motion that precisely matches the emphasis you give to your

words, like how a conductor's baton strikes the air in unison with the orchestra's punchy notes.

2. **The John Kasich:** Sounds like a deli sandwich named after the former U.S. senator from Ohio. Not quite. But it's a phenomenon not without some ham in it. During a GOP debate in 2016, Kasich tried to punctuate a point about how important encryption is in thwarting cyberattackers by karate-chopping the air with his hand over and over again. The ridiculousness of the mindless hand gesture did not go unnoticed by the writers at Comedy Central's *Daily Show*, who pounced at the opportunity to mock him. They made the clip look like a video-arcade game, superimposing flying fruit that his hands chopped into smaller pieces, each time racking up points on the screen.

   I had to replay this clip a couple of times to figure out what Kasich was saying because all I remembered was how ludicrous the repetition looked. Even if you're not victimized in a comedy sketch, that repetitive movement serves as a distraction to your audience. Instead of listening intently to what you have to say, they may instead be timing the consistent intervals in which you're making the same gesture over and over again.

3. **The Nervous Groom:** A surefire way to distract your audience from what you're saying is to allow your hands to drift above your shoulders. This is the gesticulation danger zone. I can assure you, up there, nothing good is happening. The likely culprits are all acts of nervous grooming that should have been taken care of that morning while you were getting ready, like tucking your hair behind your ear, stroking your beard, or scratching the inside of your ear, which looks like you're digging for wax. I know, ew. But that's what your audience is thinking, so scratch that itch whether it's inside your ear or anywhere near your nostril when you're offstage and out of sight.

4. **Finger Quotation Marks:** When I read comments from people who have watched presentations online, invariably the hand movement

they say they detest more than any other is when you signal that something is in quotes by bending the index and middle fingers on both hands. That gesture draws a passionate dislike from people who claim they're not even sure why. All they know is, they hate it.

WHAT DO I DO WITH MY FEET?

Ironically, it's our extremities that reflect our nervousness in the most extreme way. It's both our hands and our feet. During any public-speaking opportunity, those are the parts of your body that will betray you the quickest.

THE STATIONARY MARCH

This is the negative aspect of body language that catches most people unaware. When we're nervous standing in front of an audience, our bodies release adrenaline and other stress hormones that are triggered by our instinctive fight-or-flight response. This increases blood flow and heart rate, which causes fidgety body movements. In short, the body is trying to expel or at least dissipate our built-up tension and nervous energy. Our feet are prone to this reaction, which is why we shuffle our feet, rock back and forth, shift our weight from side to side, and aimlessly march around within a tight twelve-inch radius.

Presenting in a large venue with a big stage carries with it an element of complexity that isn't a factor when you're just standing at the head of a conference room table, one that many clients tell me is incredibly intimidating because it involves walking the stage. If the mere idea of it creates paralyzing panic, it's not the end of the world if you stay on your mark at center stage the whole time without moving. But there's no question that walking the stage in a natural way makes your presentation more dynamic, and therefore more memorable. If you do it in an awkward, choreographed way, you'll achieve the opposite effect. Here are some strategies that can help you attain the former rather than the latter result:

THE CAGED TIGER

If you move laterally back and forth onstage without ever coming to a complete stop, your movement will look like nervous pacing. When you move from point A to point B, remain stationary at point B, at least for a few sentences or until you reach the end of a thematic section. Then you can head back the other way. But perhaps instead of moving from far stage left to far stage right, you stop somewhere along the way (it doesn't have to be exactly in the middle). That decision will be based more on what you're saying than on where you're standing.

The best time to change your position onstage and move is in thematic transition. When you've finished your content on one topic and are now signaling the beginning of a different topic, that is an ideal time to walk the stage. The walk should not be some ponderous, slow slog across the stage that signals either apathy or lethargy. You should move with a sense of purpose and enthusiasm for the point you're about to make. Try to restrict your walking to the times when you're building to that next important point. Never be in transition *while* you're making the point. If for some reason you catch yourself doing it, come to an abrupt stop to finish the point. The worst thing you can do is to keep walking and look down at your feet while you're moving. This will completely mute the impact of your big idea. For those important points, you need to be rock steady, making meaningful and sustained eye contact with your audience.

DON'T SNEAK A PEEK

In a larger venue, you're likely to have confidence monitors or teleprompters just in front of the stage on the left and right sides (sometimes there may be a third in the middle). It's only natural to look at the monitor that's closest to you. But when you begin to walk to the other side of the stage, always read off the monitor you're walking toward, even though it's farther away. If you reference the one you're walking away from, the sneak peek over your shoulder will shatter the illusion that you're just up there talking and only reinforce that you're reading a script.

WHAT DO I DO WITH MY EYES?

Regardless of whether you're speaking to just four people around a conference table or four hundred in an auditorium, meaningful and sustained eye contact is crucial to making a connection with your audience. Even if you don't battle with acute cases of nerves, just about every presenter gets that shot of adrenaline that speeds up your eye movement. When you're amped up, your eyes are more likely to dart around the room, pinballing from one person to another in rapid succession. That can inhibit you from connecting with your audience. That was the finding of a 2022 study conducted in the Netherlands on how prolonged eye contact can affect the brain of the audience member.

The study found that eye contact serves as an important nonspeaking form of communication to form and maintain social connections with other people. Some evidence suggests that prolonged eye contact influences feelings of connectedness with others, strengthening bonds and opening a person's mind to trusting another.

The study suggests that any eye contact lasting longer than about five seconds may be considered prolonged. That's enough time to look at one audience member for the first half of a thought and then look toward a different person to conclude the thought.

TOSSING TO VIDEO CLIPS

I've seen many presenters sabotage themselves by creating the impression with the audience that they're not interested in their own content.

This frequently happens when video clips are played. Even though you may have already seen this clip a dozen times, you have to pretend it's the very first time you're seeing it. That means standing still in a position that is in profile to both the audience and the big screen that's behind you. I notice far too many people aimlessly wandering around the stage, killing time until the clip is over. You also don't want to turn your back on the audience to look at either video or slides. That's why the confidence monitors are in front of you.

DON'T LOSE THE SIZZLE

If the video is a "sizzle reel" (a high-energy, quick-edited montage of images), it's important that you don't let two or three seconds of "dead air" (a silent hole) hang in the room between the end of the video and the resumption of your presentation. And when you do resume, make sure your delivery is not flat and lifeless. The glaring disparity in energy, between the video and you speaking, will make it feel as though all the oxygen has been sucked out of the room. You must come out of that clip with the highest energy you can muster and then gradually adjust back to your normal level.

I NEED A DRINK

A few years ago, a friend who taught a graduate course at New York University in public relations asked me to guest-lecture to his class. I thought I came fully prepared, and I'm pretty sure no one would have thought otherwise from the first ten minutes of my presentation. But then something terrible happened. Something got caught in my throat. I have no idea what it was, but suddenly I was coughing uncontrollably. I desperately needed some water, and at that moment I realized I hadn't brought any and there was none to be had in the classroom. The only option was to make a dash to the water fountain in the hallway, which meant leaving the classroom in the middle of my talk. What an utter fiasco! This is the kind of meltdown that gives me nightmares.

From that moment on, I've never spoken in front of people without knowing the exact location of the nearest glass of water. I urge you to have my embarrassing episode be your cautionary tale. Always have water within reach. I hate to admit it, but if you were to ask any of the students from that class about my talk that night, none of them would remember anything I said, but I guarantee they'd all remember my mad sprint out of the room in search of water.

Having water nearby isn't enough, though. As a presenter, you have to know how and when to drink. I said this once to a client, who looked at me incredulously and said, "Please! Let's move on, I know how to drink water!" "No, really," I said. "There's a right way and a wrong way." I then walked over to a bottle of water on a side table and came to a dead stop in my explanation for why it's important. In complete silence, I picked up the bottle, unscrewed the cap, took a long sip, put the top back on, set the bottle back down on the table, and only then did I resume speaking. "What you just saw is *not* the way to do it if you are in front of an audience of any size." My what-not-to-do demonstration had resulted in seven seconds of dead air, ample time to lose the engagement of the audience. Then I demonstrated the right way to take a drink of water during a presentation. I continued talking all through the act of picking up the bottle, unscrewing the cap, and half-lifting it to my mouth. Then I paused for two beats to actually drink, and then I immediately resumed talking while putting the top back on and placing it back on the table.

The difference between seven lost seconds and two lost seconds is much more than five seconds. What gets lost is the energy in the room and the perception of you being in command. If you doubt me, do a web search for former Florida senator Marco Rubio's infamous water-drinking fiasco (which I referred to in the chart on page 149) during his party's televised response to President Obama's State of the Union message in 2010. During that speech, Rubio's throat got dry and he furtively reached over to a table off-camera for a tiny bottle of water. He looked ridiculous trying to sneak a quick drink of water, and because he did it all wrong, it brought his speech to a grinding halt. I imagine you'd be hard-pressed to find even the most rabid political junkies who have any recollection of what Rubio said. But I'm sure they all remember his desperate reach for the tiniest bottle of Poland Spring on the planet.

As stand-alone words of advice, not one of these tips may seem in your mind to be a difference-maker. But the whole of the guidance is greater than the sum of its parts. When I see a truly outstanding public speaker, they are not just cherry-picking a few of these strategies to work on. They are implementing nearly all of them, because they know that each one of them contributes to impressive body language that bolsters their executive presence and makes them more memorable.

DO THIS	NOT THAT
Walk the Stage During Thematic Transition	Pace Around Randomly, Never Stopping
Cease Your Hand Movements Periodically	Gesticulate in Constant/ Repetitive Motion
Keep Your Hands Below Your Shoulders	Scratch, Rub, or Touch Your Face or Head
Make Meaningful, Sustained Eye Contact	Dart Your Eyes Quickly Around the Room

PART V

FIRM UP YOUR SOFT SKILLS

In the next three chapters, your emotional intelligence (EQ) will be put to the test. That EQ plays a much bigger role than your IQ in determining whether your audience is eager to come along with you on your narrative ride. We will examine how to demonstrate empathy, how to project a likeable personality, and how to prove, through your actions, a proper respect for others.

9

EMPATHY

IT'S ALL ABOUT THEM

Therapist: "People with your condition typically have a hard time connecting with audiences."
Patient: "What condition is that?"

If there was one superpower I wished I had to make me a better public speaker, it would be the Vulcan mind meld that *Star Trek*'s Mr. Spock possesses. The ability to reach inside the mind of the other person and know exactly what they're thinking would be a nifty trick when presenting to an audience. If we really knew what they were thinking, we could make more strategically accurate adjustments on the fly to our presentations. But given that we are mere humans and not Vulcans, we are left to depend on our powers of perception and instincts to grasp whether what we have to say is engaging the audience enough to be potentially memorable. It can feel like practicing archery without a bull's-eye.

Here's the problem with that. The human face is a very deceptive window into the human mind. You may very well be captivating your audience, yet be looking out into a sea of blank faces that are sending you false signals. I've given many talks to groups where the person in the audience who looks the most checked-out is the one who comes up to me afterward to discuss the topic some more. That's why I urge you to read the room but try not to *over*read it. If you let deadpan expressions play with your head, it will adversely affect your delivery. If you listen to that evil little voice on your shoulder that whispers in your ear, "They're getting bored, get on with it!," you're likely to speed up just to get to the finish line faster. This can set off a chain reaction that can undermine your executive presence, because, as we discussed in Chapter 7, the faster you go, the more prone you are to making mistakes and the less experienced and confident you appear.

The inevitability of confronting the Dead Sea of Faces is a major reason why you need to have complete conviction within yourself that your content is top-notch. If you are intrigued, amused, and possibly even entertained by the content, you'll signal to your audience a genuine enthusiasm that can often be infectious. When you let doubt and insecurity creep in, it's likely to show in your delivery, prompting the audience to feel anxious for you. Once that dynamic takes over the room, you can kiss goodbye any chance of your message being remembered.

As you'll discover in Chapter 13, this challenge becomes even more daunting during virtual meetings. You might be able to read a room, but it's damn near impossible reading a Zoom. Any stand-up comedian will confirm that. Many during the early stages of the COVID-19 pandemic were relegated to doing their acts for virtual audiences who were either attending with their camera off, or their audio muted, or both. Without hearing audible laughter, many complained that they had no idea which parts of their material were working and which were falling flat.

LOST IN TRANSLATION

If you're presenting in a different country or to people of a different culture, you may think your in-person audience has a mute switch you can't see. This was the predicament that befell a beauty industry executive I worked with who was presenting to a group of business leaders in China. Everything she said seemed to land with a thud. The parts of her presentation that traditionally got a rise out of U.S. and European audiences were now met with blank stares. The lack of response was puzzling to her since she had done her homework in advance to learn what the audience was most interested to hear her discuss. Someone from the conference was onstage with her providing real-time translation, so it couldn't have been a lost-in-translation problem. In the absence of any logical explanation, she had a mini freak-out onstage and started stumbling through her presentation, which she had given several times in the past. It was only after the event was over that someone explained to her that audiences in China consider sitting stoically through someone's presentation to be a sign of respect.

ADVANCED INTELLIGENCE

A full scouting report on what to expect from your audience is always important, but it's especially crucial when speaking to people in a different country or from a different culture. Find out which of your typical references may go over the heads of a foreign audience and if there's something more regionally relevant to use as a replacement. This is how you make empathy work cross-border. It's also a way to demonstrate to your audience that you value them enough to take the time to understand their culture and speak to them in a way that honors their frames of reference. The opposite of empathy is self-centered arrogance, the kind of narcissism that makes people think it's okay to give the same presentation to an audience in São Paolo that you gave in San Francisco. Heck, I wouldn't even give the same presentation to that audience in San Francisco that I gave to the one in Cincinnati. You want each audience to feel that your presentation was tailor-made for them and nobody else. In fact, the first question we ask our clients is, "Who's the audience and what are they hoping to learn from you?" That's that bedrock. Everything else is built upon that. It's the first question we ask ourselves when we're preparing our own presentations.

Finding the answer to that question can be achieved in a few different ways. While more than half of the respondents in our survey said they invest time in researching who their audience will be and what matters to them, more people said they use the same presentation regardless of the audience than the number of people who rely on reading the audience.

HOW DO YOU DETERMINE WHAT YOUR AUDIENCE WANTS TO KNOW?

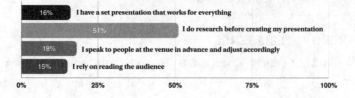

For me and my coaching colleagues at Clarity, almost every coaching session begins with a Keynote deck that imparts the communication strategies we've amassed and refined over the years. In that deck, there are five slides that speak to that particular client. Two of them incorporate the client's logo into the slide, a pretty basic addition. From there the connection with the client gets more intricate, and that intricacy requires research and information processing on our part.

SOW THEIR "BUTTON"

The third slide offers our suggestion for how the client should articulate their mission. It's rare that a company doesn't have an established mission statement, but it's even more rare when it's less than a paragraph long and actually makes sense. So we translate their long, rambling, jargon-laden statement into what we call a "button," which is a hypercondensed statement of purpose. For instance, our button is "helping people be more memorable communicators." When the client sees their reason for being through the lens of an outsider, it often produces a lightbulb moment and a response of "You're so right! In a nutshell, that *is* what we do!" Of course, there's always the possibility that someone will view this attempt of ours to define who they are not as an ultimate act of empathy, but as presumptuous arrogance. "Who the hell are you to tell us our business?" That's why I always preface the reveal of their button by saying, "Recognizing that sometimes an outsider's perspective can yield a revealing alternative, I took a crack at what a possible button for your company could be. I'm not saying this is the one and only possibility, but from the outside looking in, it seems to me that this encapsulates your purpose." I find that caveat goes a long way toward getting the client's buy-in on the suggestion.

The fourth slide reinforcing that our focus is solely on what's relevant to them, and not what we want to talk about, is a graphic showing the six areas of questioning they're most likely to face in the Q&A that follows their presentation. Like the button, this can only be crafted ahead of time after thoroughly researching their mission, narrative, key messaging, and what skeptics and competitors are saying about them on the web.

By now, you're probably realizing two undeniable truths:

1. Empathy is incredibly valuable.
2. Empathy doesn't come cheap.

It requires a commitment of time on your part to get your finger squarely on the pulse of your audience, but that effort generates an enormous return on investment and the most valuable of all commodities in a partnership, which is trust. Besides, how can you ever hope to read your audience if you don't know a little something about them?

YOU CAN'T BE WHAT YOU CAN'T SEE

The final empathy component deals with the examples you provide and the stories you tell. We show numerous video clips in our deck to demonstrate the skills that accomplished presenters possess. It is vitally important that these examples feature a diverse group of professionals, regardless of the audience you're addressing. But if you are presenting to a specialized audience, perhaps executive women or an employee resource group for Black engineers, it is doubly important to have the speakers in the videos reflect the composition of the audience. The worst thing you could do is play a handful of video clips that exclusively feature white men, holding them up as what everyone should aspire to be. Beyond just making sure there is demographic relevance to your stories and examples, be aware of what industry your audience works in. There's not much benefit to showing video examples of executives in the beauty industry if you're presenting to a group of venture capitalists.

EMPATHY REDEFINED

The dictionary definition of empathy is "the ability to understand and share the feelings of others." When that quality is absent, it's like hearing a sour note from an orchestra. One of my fellow presenters at an event at the London Stock Exchange was asked to speak on the topic of the power that digitalization holds for investor relations (IR) professionals. As the founder and managing director of an IR consulting firm, he was supposed to get up and share valuable insights into how the entire IR industry was likely to evolve and how the audience could best position themselves to prosper in this new landscape. Instead, what he provided was nothing more than a salesy pitch deck for his company that I guarantee he's given dozens of times. I'm sure of it because he delivered it in the flattest way imaginable. Nothing about it was tailored to the audience, and as a result, it held little to no value for them. With this memory still fresh in mind, I asked behavioral psychologist Adam Grant for his take on the importance of empathy.

His definition was spot-on: "Empathy shows that you're not trying to manipulate your audience—you're trying to help them." By that definition, that speaker notched an epic fail.

Grant's definition of empathy is one of the biggest driving motivations of strong communicators. MSNBC's Stephanie Ruhle, whose insights we've shared in earlier chapters, uses empathy as a grounding force. "I want to help my audience get better and smarter. If I am doing everything through that lens, and if the person I'm speaking to knows that, then I think we can have a really thoughtful conversation."

TAKE THE AUDIENCE'S PULSE

When composing a presentation, ask yourself every couple of slides, "Does this information provide useful insights that make it possible for the audience to achieve something that otherwise might not have been possible?" A five-minute presentation constructed atop a foundation of empathy is far more valuable than a twenty-minute one in which the speaker's finger is nowhere near the pulse of the audience. As much as I try to keep this in mind while putting the deck together, I never assume that I have a completely accurate read. That's why I always make a point of getting to the venue early enough to take part in either the breakfast that precedes the event's program or, if I'm speaking in the afternoon, the lunch break in the middle of day. This gives me an opportunity to work the room, and to pose two simple questions to as many people as I can: "What would you like to learn today? What's the most important and valuable insight that would make your daily life as a communicator better?" The responses you get make it possible to implement last-minute adjustments to your talk that steer it more directly to what's top of mind with your audience. Later, during my presentation, I'll sometimes even say, "I greatly enjoyed speaking to some of you at breakfast this morning, and I was really struck by how many of you mentioned [fill in the blank] as one of the most important communication skills you'd like to acquire."

Often, I don't even wait until I get to the venue to go on this intelligence-gathering mission. One time, when I was giving a talk at Netflix headquarters in Los Gatos, California, I was waiting for a ride-share outside my hotel when I struck up a casual conversation with a woman named Courtney, who was also waiting. It turned out she worked at Netflix and was going to be attending my talk. Fabulous! Why wait for the gathering-around-the-coffee-urn moment to get some valuable insights? The conversation we had driving over together was illuminating in the most valuable way. She told me that the most important communication skill she needed was how to tell a story. For all that's been written about the importance of storytelling, it is an ability many people are endlessly searching for. I told her that most stories have a basic structure. First, you need to set the scene and provide the context. Next, you need to establish the inherent tension or challenge that needs to be addressed. Finally, you need to explain the outcome, how it was all resolved, and how someone overcame obstacles or adversity. According to Paul J. Zak, the founding director of the Center for Neuroeconomics Studies and a professor of economics, psychology, and management at Claremont Graduate University, this formula will help with both motivation and persuasion since it will capture people's hearts by first stimulating their minds.

When it was my time onstage, I was able to create a quasi-ad-lib moment in which I said, "You know, I had a really interesting conversation with Courtney on the way over here this morning [pointing to her in the audience] and I was interested to learn how important the art of storytelling is in your weekly meetings." This device works. It breaks down a wall that people perceive to stand between the speaker and the audience. It also sounds like an off-the-cuff, unscripted moment, which always garners more attention. Instead of talking *at* the audience, you're now speaking *with* them.

BE A MIND READER

One of the other keys to displaying empathy is the ability to crawl inside the head of your audience and experience their emotions. Predicting how people will react to something you tell them is a skill worth improving. In fact, when you compose your presentation, constantly ask yourself, "What am I saying that can likely be met with skepticism or flat-out disagreement?" So, let's say you propose a certain course of action to resolve an issue in your company. Try to imagine what the source of resistance is likely to be when you propose this approach. Then, immediately on the heels of revealing your idea, say, "Now I know some of you are probably thinking to yourselves, how is this going to work given the company priorities we just established?" This is what allows you to transform what is essentially a monologue into a dialogue. Now you've got the makings of a conversation instead of just a presentation.

Verbalizing the anticipated feelings and emotions of your audience brings you closer to them and helps them see your point of view more clearly and remember what you say more vividly. This skill is particularly valuable when you're delivering difficult news. For instance, if you're telling a group that the resources they must work with are going to be cut, it's crucial that you acknowledge how they're likely to react to that news. You might say, "I know how difficult this must be to hear that we have to do more with less. It means all of us making certain sacrifices that are not easy to make. But every great organization, at some point in its life, faces a similar crossroads. The ones that roll up their collective sleeves and power through to create more positive momentum are the ones that ensure that their sacrifices will be short-term. I know we all want to regain our stature so that we can operate in a way that is satisfying and fulfilling to all of us."

Often it comes down to something as simple as "I feel your pain." In many observers' minds, the 1988 presidential election turned on a moment of empathy. Bill Clinton was trailing George H. W. Bush in the polls. They squared off in a town hall–style debate, sitting in seats that resembled barstools in front of an audience of regular people. Paul Begala, who along with James Carville was a key adviser to Clinton, believed that it was crucial for Clinton to connect with the struggles of the audience:

"Clinton was eager to engage the audience. In our prep sessions, as well as in the town hall itself, he sat poised on his stool like a sprinter in the starting blocks. As soon as someone asked him a question, he would engage with them, ask them a question or two, then synthesize their concerns with his own experience and his ideas for the future."

A woman asked, "How has the national debt personally affected each of your lives. And if it hasn't, how can you honestly find a cure for the economic problems of the common people if you have no experience in what's ailing them?"

President Bush stumbled. When he was finished, Clinton sprang to his feet and walked toward the woman. This exchange followed:

CLINTON: Tell me how it's affected you again. You know people who've lost their jobs and lost their homes.
WOMAN: Well, yeah, uh-huh.
CLINTON: Well, I've been governor of a small state for twelve years. I'll tell you how it's affected me. Every year, Congress and the president sign laws that makes us—make us do more things and gives us less money to do it with. I see people in my state, middle-class people, their taxes have gone up in Washington and their services have gone down

while the wealthy have gotten tax cuts. I have seen what's happened in this last four years when in my state, when people lose their jobs, there's a good chance I'll know them by their names. When a factory closes, I know the people who ran it. When the businesses go bankrupt, I know them. And I've been out here for thirteen months in meetings just like this ever since October with people like you all over America, people who have lost their jobs, lost their livelihood, lost their health insurance.

That exchange was pivotal. Clinton showed that he got it. He was empathetic as well as intellectual.

Clinton's bolt-from-the-barstool moment highlighted a couple of the characteristics empathetic people demonstrate. He actively listened to the audience member. Instead of just meeting her question with standard talking points and generic political rhetoric, he asked her a question to get a better sense of her individual situation. By contrast, Bush was caught glancing at his watch, which is the universal symbol for "How much longer do I have to endure this misery?" The stark contrast was believed to shift the momentum of the race, which, of course, Clinton won in an upset.

When you display empathy to your audience, the message they receive is that you care enough about them to understand their situation with sufficient clarity that you can offer meaningful and helpful suggestions. You are perceived to be both interesting and interested. The other qualities the audience assigns to you are keen intuition and emotional intelligence, both of which make you more engaging and, as a result, more memorable.

There's perhaps no better opportunity to demonstrate empathy than when someone asks you, "So what does your company do?" At first glance it sounds ridiculously easy. In reality, it's often the hardest question business executives face, not because they don't know, but because most have never been taught how to articulate it in a way that puts their customer first. They assume this is an invitation to just talk about themselves—the opposite of empathy.

LOOKING THROUGH THE CUSTOMER LENS

Those oblivious instincts were on full display in February 2000 when the CBS News program *60 Minutes* decided to do a story on one of the hottest tech companies in New York's Silicon Alley, Razorfish. At a valuation of $4 billion, Razorfish was a unicorn more than a dozen years before the term was invented to describe a billion-dollar startup. Because of that status, the number one news program in America wanted to do a profile, an opportunity that should have been nothing short of a multimillion-dollar marketing bonanza. In the world of earned media at that time, no other media coverage held more potential for boosting a brand's name recognition, and yet the Razorfish founders did worse than squander the opportunity. They turned the whole thing into an unmitigated disaster for one simple reason: they couldn't coherently answer the question "What do you do?"

The founders, Craig Kanarick and Jeff Dachis, answered in a vague, self-centered, and unrelatable way. "We've asked our clients to recontextualize their business," they said. "We've recontextualized what it is to be a services business."

The show's correspondent, Bob Simon, sensing meaningless, word-salad nonsense, went in for the kill: "There are people out there, such as myself, who have trouble with the word 'recontextualize.' Tell me what you do, in English."

When they continued being obtuse, Simon repeated, now with an exasperated tone, "That's still very vague. But what is it you do?" The answer did not get any more specific or empathetic: "We radically transform businesses to help invent and reinvent them," Dachis said. Finally, in Simon's narration, he had to translate what sounded like gibberish into intelligible English: "Translation? Teaching established companies how to make more money and reach more customers through the internet," then adding in a snarky tone, "or something like that."

This lack of awareness that it is *always* about the audience and not about you is pervasive in the professional world. Most companies mistakenly try to describe themselves as a thing, and often it sounds something like "We're an omni-channel, fully integrated, brand-agnostic platform scaling solutions across multiple verticals for the enterprise." If I were to take that buzzword-laden, abstract, say-nothing approach to my own company, this is the garbled mess I'd likely settle on: "We're a global firm leveraging journalistic know-how across the entire media ecosystem, to provide best-in-class communications solutions."

This doesn't tell an audience anything useful. In fact, from this theoretical definition, nobody can tell whether we're a communications coaching firm or a telecom. But if you get outside your own head and make your consumer, customer, or client the focal point of your definition, what you come up with is what I call an experiential definition: "If you had a big media interview, presentation, or speech coming up, you would come to us for coaching and prep that could help you capitalize on that opportunity." Opting for the experiential approach directly and proactively answers the questions "What problem do you solve for me? How, when, and why would I engage with you?" In telling your story, you need to be answering their questions. Ironically, the more empathetic you are, the more subtly promotional you'll be.

One of the most effective ways to inject a sense of empathy into your professional relationships, whether you are actively collaborating on a project with a client or merely pitching your services to them, is to swap out two simple words. Instead of saying "you," say "we," as in "What if we were to try this approach?" or "Are we likely to be open to criticism if we move forward with this plan?" Making this easy change positions you as a partner who is fully invested in the client's organizational success.

LISTEN CLOSELY, LISTEN ACTIVELY

Without truly listening to others, empathy is impossible. Unfortunately, for many, the times they should be listening are conflated with the time they spend waiting their turn until they can hear themselves talk again.

Jen Psaki, host of MSNBC's *Inside with Jen Psaki* and former White House press secretary to President Joe Biden and press aide to President Obama, believes that one of the key ingredients to empathy is focused listening.

"Another important quality is listening and the best communicators are listening for clues on how to better connect with the audience they are engaging with whether that is one person or much larger."

Research shared by Character Lab, which was cofounded by Angela Duckworth, a psychology professor at the University of Pennsylvania and author of the *New York Times* bestselling book *Grit*, supports the importance of active listening. Their work suggests that healthy interpersonal relationships share three essential elements. The first is *understanding*—seeing the other person for who they are, including their desires, fears, strengths, and weaknesses. The second is *validation*—valuing the other person's perspective, even if it differs from your own. And the third is *caring*—expressing authentic affection, warmth, and concern.

The expression of concern that Duckworth cites is critical to being in an empathetic mindset when you present to an audience. Keep in mind, this is made more difficult by assorted technology that erect interpersonal barriers between you and your audience, not the least of which are Zoom, which we will discuss in Chapter 13, and PowerPoint, which we deal with in Chapter 12.

DO THIS	NOT THAT
Help Your Audience Get Smarter/Better	Lecture on Your Point of View
Cite Aspirational Examples That Are Culturally Diverse	Showcase Homogeneous Examples of Communication Role Models
Describe What You Do in Terms of the Problems You Solve for Others	Describe Yourself Theoretically in a Way That Puts You First
Listen Attentively in Order to Learn	Don't View Listening as Waiting Your Turn to Talk Again

10

IT'S ALL ABOUT LIKEABILITY

"Your content and delivery are pretty good, but you're making Larry David seem lovable."

Stop ten people on the street and ask them what makes someone likeable, and don't be surprised if you get ten different answers. Of all the subjects we examine in this book, likeability is perhaps the most elusive to explain and difficult to describe in precise terms. It's a little like what U.S. Supreme Court justice Potter Stewart said while ruling on a case involving free speech. He would not profess to clearly define obscenity, but "I know it when I see it."

The quest to identify what constitutes likeability, from our experience, is a crucial discovery for a couple of key reasons:

1. Being likeable perhaps opens more doors of opportunity in life than any other quality.
2. Presenting yourself as likeable to an audience dramatically increases

their engagement, and therefore the likelihood they will remember what you say. With greater recall of what you say, there's a greater chance that your words will serve to persuade and influence.

Likeability is inherently subjective. People tend to see others as likeable when they demonstrate qualities that they themselves possess or they see as desirable. If you're an animal lover, you naturally view someone who is kind to animals as likeable. If you encounter someone who is not conversationally selfish and shows a genuine interest in others, then you will likely find them likeable if that's a quality you admire. This is what a study reported by the NIH calls the fundamental principle of liking (FPL).

Likeability plays a major role when job applicants are pitching themselves for an open position. When I was in my early twenties, I applied for a job as an associate producer on a TV news program that I desperately wanted because it represented a "big-break" career opportunity. To improve my chances of getting the job, I polished and repolished my writing samples. I watched the show and made observational notes about the production quality so I would have a point of view if asked. I developed two questions to ask the person interviewing me for the job (because you should never, *ever* come empty-handed, without your own questions). I was convinced that all those efforts were instrumental in landing me the job, until a few months later when I decided to ask my boss why he chose me and not someone else. "Was it the quality of my writing samples that pushed me over the top? Was it my production feedback? Was it my previous newsroom experience?" I asked him. His response was a bit deflating. "Not really. I just figured you were a nice, likeable kid who wouldn't give me any shit." So much for qualifications.

At my company, we have a strict hiring policy we call ONP, which stands for "only nice people." Yes, they need to have the right experience and qualifications, but ultimately, we exist in an industry in which mastery of the softer, social skills is mandatory. Clients must hear in the way we communicate to them that we genuinely care about their welfare and are 100 percent committed to their professional development. To determine if candidates have this quality, we ask ourselves, "Are we going to look forward to spending more than eight hours a day, several times a week with this person?" If the answer if yes, that person is well on their way to getting hired. This criterion is more important than you may think.

THE BUDDIES ON THE BUS

In an article in *Forbes*, Carol Kinsey Goman, a PhD, told a story of a recent graduate who landed a job at one of the prestigious tech companies of Silicon Valley. The woman told Goman that she believed she was hired out of a large pool of impressive candidates because she passed the "sit next to on a bus" test.

In this candidate's mind, there are two types of job applicants. The first are those who are so brilliant and talented, they are hired on the spot. The rest of us, while not as brilliant, are all smart and capable, but we also seem like the type of person you would enjoy sitting next to on a long bus ride. In other words, we're likeable. This factors into everything, from the hiring processes at the smallest companies in the world, to the election of the most powerful person in the world. In presidential politics, hundreds of millions of dollars are spent analyzing how to make a candidate more likeable. Those who cover politics believe that for many voters, policy particulars take a back seat to the question of whom they would rather have a beer with.

Paul Begala, one of the strategic masterminds of Bill Clinton's 1988 successful run for the White House, marveled at how likeability was a quality that Clinton never had to work at.

"As far as likeability, I believe in interactional synchrony. You get what you give. People like Bill Clinton because he likes them. He is the smartest person I have ever met, but he never acts like he's the smartest person in the room, because he truly never believes he is. He believes everyone has a story that is different from his, and he can learn from everyone. So he is genuinely interested, genuinely concerned, genuinely empathetic. The test is not really "Who would I like to have a beer with?" It is "Who should raise my kids if my spouse and I die? Who understands my life, shares my values, and cares about me?"

Jonathan Lemire, part of MSNBC's *Morning Joe* team, interviews people every morning who are single-minded in their goal of saying things that stick with the viewing audience. He believes that likeability is tied to engagement:

"When someone comes off as likeable, they come off as charismatic, they come off as decent, they come off as thoughtful, they come off as someone whom I wouldn't mind just hanging out with. I think someone who comes across as genuine and decent is more likely to grab my attention than someone who seems like deeply programmed."

Lemire's MSNBC colleague Stephanie Ruhle agrees that coming across as too slick or too messaged compromises a person's likeability:

"I honestly think it all goes back to vulnerability. To me, likeability is vulnerability. It's not, that person's so funny, that person's so good-looking, that person's so cool. It's the person who's willing to be quirky and honest."

PLAY TO WIN

So many people obsessively focus on getting a talk or presentation right that they lose sight of the importance of coming across as likeable. When you mistakenly make the absence of mistakes the ultimate goal, the result is likely to be a flat presentation that fails to be memorable for the right reasons. This is the public-speaking equivalent of "playing not to lose" instead of playing to win. I would much rather you take the pressure off yourself to be perfect, or mistake-free, and instead focus on letting your enthusiasm shine through for the value that your information holds for the audience. You must display a sense of personal fulfillment in knowing you're helping those listening to you. When you make this motivation your center of gravity, your demeanor is brighter, and you come across as more likeable.

In our survey, 65 percent deemed likeability as either an important or very important quality to exhibit when presenting. While that number may seem high, that means 35 percent consider it either not important or not crucial. That is a lot of people who are missing out on wielding one of the most secret weapons of persuasion in public speaking.

HOW IMPORTANT IS IT THAT YOU BE SEEN AS LIKEABLE WHEN YOU PRESENT?

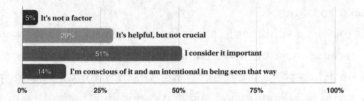

THE SECRET WEAPON OF LIKEABILITY

As a presenter, never underestimate the power of a smile. It is a vital tool in convincing your audience that you're enjoying the opportunity to speak with them and provide insights and information that are helpful. When you are consumed by the play-not-to-lose mentality, mustering a smile can be difficult because the pressure of being perfect has likely stripped the joy out of the equation. A natural, warm smile is also the greatest cloaking device ever for a bad case of nerves. In my experience, it's rare to see someone smile who is extremely nervous. So, if you are one of the many people who are terrified by public speaking, realize there is a virtuous cycle that you have the power to set into motion, but also realize this might be a fake-it-till-you-make-it scenario.

The first turn of the wheel on this virtuous cycle is your smile. It all starts there. Upon the audience first encountering you, a primal reaction occurs in which they make a determination as to whether you are friend or foe. Once your smile convinces them of your friend status, the next turn of the wheel happens: they relax and become more receptive to what you have to say. The energy in the room created by that receptiveness leads to the third turn in the virtuous cycle—your heightened relaxation that stems from the confidence that your well-prepared, well-rehearsed presentation is resonating and being appreciated. The more revolutions this cycle makes, the less nervous you will be. This is how people overcome what to this day remains the number one fear in life: public speaking.

This may be a skill that requires intentional focus and work to acquire, because most of us are completely unaware of the vibe we're giving off when we present to others. We may think we're displaying a neutral facial expression and demeanor, but that's often not the case. When I show my clients the video recording of the practice run of their speech or presentation, I hold back and wait for them to remark on the warmth of their demeanor. More times than not, they say, "Wow, I look kind of angry." We call this RBF. No, not *that* RBF. That's so 2013. For us, RBF stands for "resting bothered face." This presents a big hurdle for presenters in their efforts to be heard and remembered. In fact, a 2017 study from the NIH indicates that angry faces cause the most brain activation or arousal in the listener due to the perceived threat they create. The problem is, this is not an engagement arousal, this is a flight arousal. The study also indicated that angry faces inhibit working memory, especially in older adults. So, if your goal is to be memorable, ditch the RBF, as our survey clearly illustrates:

DO YOU FIND LIKEABLE
SPEAKERS MORE MEMORABLE?

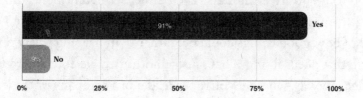

Once you've acknowledged the importance of a smile, embrace the notion that when you smile is a critical consideration in coming across as authentic and sincere. In our survey, fewer than 35 percent gave the correct answer when asked when they smile during a presentation. For your smiling to be viewed as relatable and appropriate, it has to be synced with the delivery of an upbeat message or good news. To confine that display of warmth for only the beginning when you're introduced falls short of what's needed, and to smile all throughout the presentation, regardless of the message you're delivering, can come across as slick, insincere, or, even worse, creepy.

WHEN DO YOU SMILE WHEN YOU PRESENT?

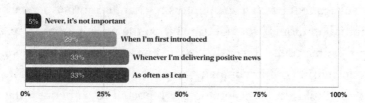

Right about now you may be silently saying to me, "Hey, Bill, a lot of times I have to present news that's not great, news about teams underperforming and falling short of established goals. How do you expect me to smile through that?" That point is well taken. It would be bizarre to smile when sharing disappointing news. But likeable people tend to be positive thinkers. Even amid disappointment, they are adept at communicating in an upbeat manner, focusing on the possibilities of how good things could be, rather than harping solely on the problem that needs fixing. That's just a more effective and inspirational approach anyway, whether you're the leader of a company or the leader of the free world.

Jay Carney, who back in Chapter 4 extolled the virtues of Barack Obama's comedic timing, also admired how his displays of warmth were well timed. "Obama has . . . a great smile. And when you use it at the right moment, it's incredibly disarming and reinforces the point you're making and the truth that you're telling or that you're trying to persuade an audience of."

BRIGHT FROM START

As we mentioned earlier, we fully subscribe to the belief that there's no take two on first impressions. The problem is, science disagrees. You do indeed have an opportunity to neutralize a bad first impression, but it's a tough task. According to a Harvard study, it typically takes eight subsequent positive encounters to change another person's negative initial opinion of you. Getting off on the wrong foot can be costly. With this in mind, I recently coached an executive who was having another division of her company brought under her supervision. Hundreds of employees, who previously reported to someone they liked, were now going to report to her. Our goal was for her to get off on the right foot by projecting both competence and warmth, and having those two qualities be in a harmonious balance. According to a 2023 Science Direct study, those are the predominant characteristics she will be first judged on by her new reports. The author of the study, Harvard associate professor Amy Cuddy, acknowledges that while it might be ideal to be both "feared and loved," warmth and trustworthiness are more important. Why does the science give even greater importance to likeability and warmth over competence? The reason, according to Cuddy's analysis, published in the *Harvard Business Review*, is that it is extremely rare for leaders who are disliked to be deemed effective. In fact, when they examined over 50,000 leaders, only 27 of them ranked low on likeability and high on leadership effectiveness. It's hard to argue with that correlation. That's why Cuddy characterizes warmth as the "conduit of influence": because it engenders trust and communication. That's why my client's introduce-myself-to-the-staff presentation kicked off with some insights as to who she is as a person: her family, her pets, her love of the outdoors, etc. She placed a lot of stock in the importance of likeability and it's already paying dividends.

HOW TO BE MORE LIKEABLE

Maintaining that equilibrium between confidence and warmth is a delicate balancing act. To determine what constitutes the proper mix, both on initial impression and how it plays out over time, social psychologists Michael Dufner and Sascha Krause conducted a study in 2023 in which they assembled small groups of young adults who did not know one another. They spent a brief time engaging with each group member individually. Researchers watched each interaction and classified the test subjects into one of two categories. The first group demonstrated what were called "agentic" behaviors, which are confidence, dominance, and slight boastfulness. The other displayed "communal" behaviors, which are characterized by politeness, warmth, friendliness, and benevolence. When it came to initial likeability, those who displayed high levels of both agentic and communal behaviors were better liked. But when it came to establishing a deeper and lasting connection, only the communal behavior mattered. Those qualities that contribute to likeability were what determined whether people wanted to form a friendship with the other person. What the study indicates is that initially we might be impressed by confidence or maybe even slight boastfulness. It can increase liking. But likeability is what inspires us to get to know people better and potentially care about them.

THE "MADE IN CHINA" CEO

What happens if you can't find a CEO candidate who has the right balance of argentic and communal behaviors? Well, if you're a tech-savvy firm in China, you make one through artificial intelligence. That's exactly what the firm Netdragon did when they created an avatar to be the head of the company. They named her Tang Yu. Her creators' intent was to infuse her with a personality that employees would hopefully see as kind, yet with the seriousness that's required of a top executive. Because she's a creation of AI, she knows every detail of the company's six thousand employees and can therefore render decisions on raises and promotions that are deemed completely objective and fact-based. This, of course, raises the question whether likeability in the future will be a programmed or genetically modified quality. We'll look deeper into the implications of AI's impact on how we communicate in Chapter 14.

DO THIS	NOT THAT
Show Warmth Toward Your Audience	Exhibit a Serious Demeanor That Looks Dour
Communal Behaviors	Agentic Behaviors
Remain Upbeat and Inspirational	Seem Overwhelmed by Negative News
Play to Win	Play Not to Lose

11

MANSPLAINING, MANTERRUPTING, AND THEFTOSTERONE

"Listen Todd. I've been mansplained to by the best of them
and your condescension needs some serious work."

Since the beginning of time, men have sought to exert control and dominance over women. Nowhere is this fact more obvious than in a professional environment, when men and women are communicating. It happens in one-on-one conversations. It happens in meetings. Women express an opinion or put forth an idea, and men, either intentionally or unwittingly, undermine them, or worse, copy them and abscond with the credit. There are four ways this can occur: mantimidation, mansplaining, manterrupting, and one that I've coined: theftosterone.

1. **Mantimidation:** A physical act of aggression by a man to establish dominance and authority over a woman, like invading her sense of personal space to rattle her or get her to take a step back and retreat.

    Salt-in-the-Wound Component: If after being called out on the unacceptable nature of his behavior, the man plays the victim card and whines that his freedoms and his rights are being trampled.

PLAYING OUT IRL (IN REAL LIFE)

If you watched the second debate of the 2016 presidential campaign between Hillary Clinton and Donald Trump, you saw a blatant example of attempted mantimidation, during which Trump kept hovering over Clinton when she had the floor. Reflecting back on the episode, Clinton wrote, "We were on a small stage and no matter where I walked, he followed me closely, staring at me, making faces. It was incredibly uncomfortable. He was literally breathing down my neck. My skin crawled."

Clinton recognized she had two options. She could call him on his antics and tell him to back off, that she couldn't be intimidated, or she could try to look unfazed, remain smiling, and carry on as if it weren't happening. She said she chose the latter because many years of men trying to throw her off her game had conditioned her to respond that way. She wondered whether she overlearned the lesson of staying calm and biting her tongue.

Knowing how prone Trump has always been toward mantimidation, I'm surprised Clinton's advance debate team hadn't prepared for that contingency. Just two days earlier, the infamous *Access Hollywood* tape was made public, the one in which Trump is heard bragging about grabbing and groping women. Put those two factors together (his bullying propensities and the scandalous tape) and you have the perfect justification for a back-pocket zinger Clinton could have pulled out. Among her options could have been the following technique.

BLOCKING THE PUNCH

"Two days ago, the whole country heard you admit to molesting women—now you're stalking me onstage . . . you just don't get it, do you, Donald?" Or she could have dismissively said, "Oh Donald, act your age. You're lurking behind me like some pathetic grade-school bully. Go stand in your corner until you're called on."

. Who knows how either could have changed the dynamic of the race. By not challenging him, Clinton relinquished her power to Trump, who amid a major scandal desperately needed an infusion of some. The rule of the schoolyard is, when a bully pushes you, you push them back harder to send a message that you can't be intimidated. Staying silent merely encourages these perpetrators to repeat this repugnant behavior, either with you or another woman they encounter in a work setting. Perhaps most importantly, Trump's lurking presence was the lasting impression, the memorable moment, not Clinton rightfully putting him in his place.

OUT OF THE SPOTLIGHT

Recently a female partner at an asset management firm came to us for presentation training, but early in the session it became clear what she really wanted to learn most were some skills on how to handle episodes of mantimidation that had already been inflicted on her several times. Due to a very youthful appearance that defied her extensive professional experience, male clients and prospective investors were regularly calling her qualifications into question. We asked her to send us the rude and potentially intimidating comments men had made to her, so we could craft some effective retorts. The responses needed to strike the delicate balance between standing up to these misogynists in response to their inappropriate remarks, and not ruining the business relationship. Here are the comments she sent us. Next to them is our counsel on how to respond in the future:

Blocking the Punch

THE MANTIMIDATING OFFENSE	THE SUGGESTED COMEBACK
"I can't believe they sent a junior analyst to this meeting."	"Well, one quick look at my bio would have told you I have a wealth of experience."
"You're really younger than expected."	"Well, I guess I have my parents to thank for those youthful genes. My ID tells a different story."
"I was expecting someone older."	"Well, today I get a chance to prove that being capable and experienced has little to do with age."
"I thought your boss was going to be joining."	"They don't need to. They have one hundred percent confidence in my abilities, just like you will when this meeting is over."
"You seem really young to have such a senior role."	"Well, you know what they say about high achievers! I know you didn't necessarily mean it that way, but I'll take that as a compliment."

Although the content of these replies may vary, the delivery needs to be consistently calm, composed, and matter-of-fact. Your tone should be professional and firm, rather than personal and flustered, because men are quick to accuse women of getting hysterical. No matter which one fits your personality, they are all intended to fire a warning shot across the bow of your boorish counterpart, signaling to them that you have every intention of standing your ground and holding your own. You could consider a couple of these comebacks a bit cheeky, a strategy many women have found works. Gretchen Whitmer, the governor of Michigan, has a lot of experience with men disrespecting her. In her political memoir, *True Gretch*, she maintains that the best way to disarm a bully is by turning insults into humor.

Madeleine Albright was skilled at that. As the first woman to serve as U.S. secretary of state, she was no stranger to being dissed, even by men who were nowhere near as accomplished as she was. Once during a press conference, a male reporter asked her the inconceivably tacky and disrespectful question, "With all due respect, don't you think you're a little too short to be a secretary of state?" It's as if including "with all due respect" somehow made it any less demeaning. Instead of letting the reporter bait her into an angry or emotional response, Albright responded with humor: "Well, I wear heels. Higher ones than usual—just to remind myself that I can always go higher."

In the tech world, when women tech founders look to raise financing from predominantly male venture capital firms, they are often met with eyes that glaze over and more questions about the downside risks than the upside potential. Those were the findings of Julia Boorstin, CNBC's senior media and technology reporter, when she was conducting research for her book *When Women Lead*. Also alarming was Boorstin's discovery that male investors had no qualms about professing ignorance about the validity of a female entrepreneur's idea for a company.

> *Many of the women I interviewed who were focused on companies serving female consumers said that the male VCs they were pitching to said they couldn't understand the company because it was not a need they had themselves. At least a dozen women told me that VCs said they should ask their wives, daughters, or assistants if the company the women were pitching made sense. Here were professionals armed with data and pitch decks, being told that their pitches couldn't be evaluated with their standard measures of addressable market and potential growth, but whether the women in their office "got it."*

To get a sense of how frequently mantimidation occurs, our Clarity Media Group survey asked both men and women how often they witness a woman at work being subjected to some form of intimidation from a male colleague. Forty percent answered it was occasionally, while only 20 percent said never.

HOW FREQUENTLY HAVE YOU WITNESSED A MAN TRY TO INTIMIDATE A FEMALE COLLEAGUE AT WORK, EITHER SUBTLY OR OVERTLY?

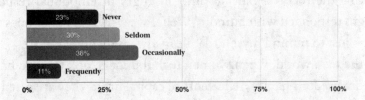

2. **Mansplaining:** When a man offers an uninvited explanation to a woman in a condescending way that assumes she knows nothing about the subject, in order to exert authority over the woman.

    Salt-in-the-Wound Component: When the woman being lectured is an expert on the topic.

PLAYING OUT IRL (IN REAL LIFE)

When Rebecca Solnit wrote an essay in 2008 titled "Men Explain Things to Me: Facts Didn't Get in Their Way," she touched a nerve. The story she told of a man interrupting her at a party to tell her about a book she absolutely must read (that book being one that Solnit herself had written) went viral, sounding all too familiar to women who have been enduring this type of condescension since the beginning of time. Within two years that phenomenon would earn the label "mansplaining," declared by the *New York Times* the Word of the Year.

You might assume that the frequency of this aggression has gone down in the years that followed. Unfortunately, you would be wrong. The number of occasions women in the workplace are subjected to this indignity has not abated. A 2022 survey of 2,000 women commissioned by *Self* found that the average woman gets mansplained to six times a week. That's more than the number of workdays there are in a week.

This aggression manifests itself in a number of ways in the workplace. These examples were compiled by the artificial intelligence platform Yoodli, based on situations that have been fed into its models:

- As a woman opens up about an experience she had, a man interrupts her to inform her that he's "faced worse."
- During a conversation while a woman discusses a current event, a man cuts her off to say she's mistaken or doesn't know what she's talking about.
- When a woman describes her position to a man, he interrupts her midsentence to inform her that he "knows how that works."
- When a woman is working on a task, a man steps in and completely takes over, even though she didn't ask for that.
- When a woman is sharing about a novel she recently read, a man cuts her off to say that she's wrong about how the book ended.

STRESS AS A TRIGGER

Interestingly, the more high-stakes the situation, the more likely mansplaining is to occur. Those were the findings of a study published by the American Psychological Association in 2012. Research conducted jointly by Harvard Business School and Wharton found that we are even more likely to fall prey to biases in high- rather than low-stakes situations. Under stress, the brain processes information less rationally, thus increasing our likelihood of relying on stereotypes.

That may help explain why one of the most flagrant instances of mansplaining happened during a 1984 vice presidential debate between George H. W. Bush and Congresswoman Geraldine Ferraro, the first female vice presidential nominee of a major party. The first gender-driven slight came when Bush referred to his Democratic opponent not as Congresswoman Ferraro, but as "Mrs. Ferraro," clearly a dig at her decision not to take her husband's last name, Zaccaro. It got worse from there. Ferraro criticized some of the CIA's secret operations, which appeared to have irked Bush, a former CIA director.

"This is serious business," Bush lectured his opponent. "But let me help you, Mrs. Ferraro, with the difference between Iran and the embassy in Lebanon." Bush went on to give what he no doubt thought was a master class in foreign policy, but in reality was the height of condescension. While he was doing that, Ferraro did what all candidates in a debate are taught to do when they are being attacked: look down and take notes. This keeps them from looking like they're just standing there, helplessly absorbing body blows from their opponent. When it was her turn to talk, Ferraro did something that was strategically crucial before a single word came out of her mouth: she gave a slight smile. Why is this so important? Because women are unjustly relegated to living in a damned-if-you-do, damned-if-you-don't world. If they let an aggression like that go unanswered, they're labeled a weak pushover. If they stick up for themselves, they're often called nasty, or worse. In addition, a smile helps convey that you are incredulously bemused by the aggressor's absurd and ridiculous behavior, rather than mortally wounded by it. This is the same advice I give in Q&A coaching when people are likely to face aggressive questioning. A wry smile takes the sting out of a brass-knuckles question. It's core to this key strategy: the more aggressive and accusatory the question, the brighter your demeanor should be. Ferraro's smile made her comeback that much more effective:

"Let me just say, first of all, that I almost resent, Vice President Bush, your patronizing attitude that you have to 'teach me' about foreign policy." Over the sound of applause from the audience, she continued. "I've been a member of Congress for six years. I was there when the embassy was held hostage in Iran. I have been there, and I have seen what has happened in the past several months, seventeen months with your administration."

Ferraro's response does not reflect what typically happens in every-day occurrences of mansplaining, where according to our Clarity Media Group survey, 30 percent of the time the offense goes unchallenged.

WHEN MEN INTERRUPT TO MANSPLAIN TO WOMEN, WHAT'S THE RESPONSE?

31%	They try to ignore it and move on
28%	They ignore it in the meeting, but make their displeasure known later
27%	They confront the interruptor, without hiding their displeasure
14%	They try to be firm but pleasant while calling them on it

0%   25%   50%   75%   100%

It's hard to determine how much Ferraro's comeback was responsible for the lasting impact it had on George H. W. Bush, but years after that exchange, Bush told a reporter from the *Washington Post* that his debate with Ferraro was the lowest moment in the worst time in his career.

3. **Manterrupting:** When a man doesn't allow a woman to finish her thought and conversationally bulldozes her in midsentence to diminish her status and monopolize the conversation.

   Salt-in-the-Wound Component: When the man's interruption is a complete non sequitur to the topic being discussed.

PLAYING OUT IRL (IN REAL LIFE)

On September 13, 2009, Radio City Music Hall in New York City was the scene of what could very well be the most famous episode of man-terrupting in recent history. Nineteen-year-old Taylor Swift had just heard her name announced as the winner of the Moon Man Award for the Best Female Video at the MTV Music Awards. Her level of shock over beating out the likes of Beyoncé, Kelly Clarkson, Lady Gaga, Katy Perry, and Pink was only to be outdone by what happened when she stepped up to the microphone. After thanking everyone and admitting she had dreamed of someday winning a VMA award, an uninvited nightmare stormed the stage. An angry Kanye West grabbed the microphone away from Swift, saying, "I'm really happy for you, I'll let you finish, but Beyoncé had one of the best videos of all time."

This brazen act of manterrupting left the audience stunned, Beyoncé incredulous, and Taylor Swift speechless. As crazy as Kanye behaves, does anyone really think that he would have had the audacity to pull a stunt like that with someone like Eminem? I tend to doubt it. Of course, karma has a funny way of settling the score. The only time Taylor Swift gets interrupted these days is when her adoring "Swifties" chant her name so loud during concerts in jam-packed stadiums that she has to wait to begin the next song. And what's up with Kanye? Now *he's* the one getting interrupted, by sponsors like Adidas, who finally lost patience with his toxicity and pulled the plug on a partnership deal that was worth hundreds of millions of dollars.

THE DATA BACKS IT UP

Anecdotally, it certainly seems as though men interrupt women in work meetings more than the reverse is true. But is there data to back that up? Do women interrupt other women with the same frequency? In 2014, empirical linguist Kieran Snyder decided to find out. She conducted an informal experiment in which she sat in on work meetings that had at least four attendees. She charted how often interruptions happened, who was the interrupter, and who was the interrupted. Snyder found that men interrupted twice as often as women, and when men did the interrupting, they did it to women three times more than they did it to other men. For women, the trend is exactly the opposite. When women interrupted, 87 percent of the time they did it to other women.

Over time, studies show that women learn how to lessen their chance of being interrupted by adopting male speech patterns, such as forgoing pleasantries like "excuse me."

On matters of this nature, we would like to think that as a society, we've made progress. But the conclusions of the 2014 study are remarkably consistent with the findings of a 1975 study by University of California, Santa Barbara, sociologists Don Zimmerman and Candace West. Their sample size in evaluating interruptions by men and women during conversations was relatively small, but it was nevertheless revealing. The laboratory for their experiment was very different. They examined the phenomenon in everyday locations like coffee shops and drugstores. They chronicled thirty-one different two-person conversations they encountered and recorded them. The results couldn't have been more lopsided. In mixed-sex conversations, men were responsible for all but one of the forty-eight interruptions they overheard. That means of all the interruptions, men were guilty of 97.9 percent. The data shows that what happens in the boardroom is merely a reflection of what happens in the living room and in our broader society.

With regards to frequency in the workplace, our Clarity Media Group survey found that the percentage of respondents who witnessed manterrupting, either sometimes or frequently, exceeded 61 percent.

HOW OFTEN IN MEETINGS OR PRESENTATIONS DO YOU SEE MEN INTERRUPT WOMEN?

This propensity to interrupt women also has a tendency to pop up in the most ironic of situations. At the South by Southwest festival in 2015, Megan Smith, the chief technology officer of the United States, was taking part in a panel discussion on innovation in the technology sector. She was sharing the stage with Google executive chairman Eric Schmidt and Walter Isaacson, author of a bestselling biography of Apple cofounder Steve Jobs. As if on some surreal cue, when the subject of the conversation turned to creating more equal opportunity for women to advance their careers in the tech sector, Isaacson and Schmidt kept interrupting Smith when she was trying to speak. It got so bad that an audience member asked the two men if they were even aware that they were doing it.

VEEP DEBATE PTSD

Thirty-six years after the Bush-Ferraro debate, history came close to repeating itself when Mike Pence and Kamala Harris squared off for a debate. Like Bush, Pence was the sitting vice president, and like Ferraro, Harris was a female member of Congress, in her case senator. During the debate, Harris was poking holes in Pence's claim that the administration responded too slowly to COVID in order to keep Americans calm. When Pence tried to interrupt her, Harris was quick to stand her ground. "Mr. Vice President, I'm speaking," she said. Stopping Pence in his tracks right there was more critical than anyone at that moment could have imagined, because Harris was in the process of teeing up a memorable moment from the debate. Had she let Pence bulldoze her, she never would have had the chance to be memorable. Due to Pence's interruption, the debate moderator granted Harris fifteen more seconds to finish her answer, and she made the most of it, playing off Pence's choice of the word "calm."

"I want to ask the American people: How calm were you when you were panicked about where you were going to get your next roll of toilet paper?" Harris asked, looking directly into the camera. "How calm were you when your kids were sent home from school and you didn't know when they could go back? How calm were you when your children couldn't see your parents because you were afraid they could kill them?" The only other contender for most memorable moment that night was the black fly that decided to take up residence on Pence's white hair for what seemed like an eternity.

Those extra seconds resulted in a direct, empathetic question straight to the audience that was reminiscent of one of the most memorable moments in debate history: Ronald Reagan asking the American people during his debate with President Jimmy Carter in 1980, "Are you better off than you were four years ago?" The takeaway? You can't be memorable or captivate an audience if you allow yourself to be shut down by someone else.

OBJECTION, YOUR HONOR!

It doesn't matter how smart or accomplished women are, men still conversationally steamroll them. This is even true in the highest court in the land. An empirical study titled "Justice, Interrupted: The Effect of Gender, Ideology, and Seniority at Supreme Court Oral Arguments," conducted by Tonja Jacobi and Dylan Schweers, showed that male Supreme Court justices interrupt the female justices approximately three times as often as they interrupt each other during oral arguments. Even men who are presenting their cases before the bench interrupt the female justices, something that the court's rules forbid them to do. This is a pattern that has not let up over time. Transcripts of fifteen years of Supreme Court oral arguments show that as more women have joined the court, male justices have increased their interruptions of the female justices. Many male justices interrupt female justices at double-digit rates per term, but the reverse is almost never true. During a twelve-year span, during which women made up, on average,

24 percent of the bench, 32 percent of interruptions were *of* the female justices, but only 4 percent were *by* the female justices. Strangely, as the gender imbalance on the court has lessened over the past several years, the incidents of manterrupting have not gone down. In fact they've increased.

4. **Theftosterone:** When a woman shares an idea with her colleagues, perhaps in a meeting, and later, a man says almost the exact same thing, posing it as his own original idea in an effort to bolster his professional reputation at the expense of hers.

    Salt-in-the-Wound Component: This aggression is exacerbated when the collective response to the woman is lackluster but the man gets credit for "his" great suggestion and is all too happy to bask in the praise without the slightest sense of guilt.

PLAYING OUT IRL (IN REAL LIFE)

On occasion, television commercials provide astute commentary on the absurdities of workplace culture. Perhaps one of the best belongs to FedEx. Years ago, they produced an ad showing a group of men sitting around a conference table at work. At the head of it is a square-jawed CEO type who challenges his team to come up with proposals for how the company can cut costs. The youngest employee at the table, looking insecure and hesitant, offers a suggestion: "We could open an account on fedex.com and save ten percent on online express shipping." Four seconds of awkward silence ensue, during which his colleagues anxiously await the boss's reaction. Finally, the empty-suit CEO decisively leans forward, chiming in: "Okay, how about this? We open an account on fedex.com and save ten percent on online express shipping." The suggestion is met with a chorus of sycophantic approval from everyone at the table, except the young employee, who looks like his pocket has just been picked. He then gets up the gumption to call out his boss on the blatant theft of his idea. "You just said the same thing I did, only you did this," he says, waving his hands in a side-to-side gesture. Without a hint of shame, and not even looking in the direction of his young report, the CEO dismissively says, "No, I did this," moving his hand in an up-and-down gesture. This commercial spoofed a very real act of corporate larceny that occurs with frequency in offices all over the world. Only in this instance, the victim was a young man. In reality, this not-so-petty thievery is perpetrated on women far more often. It's what I call "theftosterone," the flagrant swiping of a woman's idea or suggestion by a man who claims it's his own and unapologetically takes credit. Like manterruptions, this also happens in matters of the Supreme Court of the United States. Theftosterone is something Justice Sonia Sotomayor sees frequently: "Most of the time women say things and they are not heard in the same way as men who might say the identical thing."

Experts believe the roots of this problem run deep. Deborah Tannen, professor of linguistics at Georgetown, has studied how men and women communicate in the workplace. Her theory is that men and women carry over communication tendencies from their formative years.

"Research by anthropologists and sociologists finds that among boys, language is used to maintain and negotiate status in the group. One way a boy gains status is by taking center stage and holding it by talking: giving information, telling stories, boasting. Among girls, it is frowned upon for a girl to seek center stage in these ways."

In later years, these aggressions are communication weapons that men use to assert greater control and dominance over women. Despite all the professional gains women have made over the past twenty years, episodes of workplace mistreatment, of which theftosterone is a form, have increased 20 percent.

When we asked those in our survey for their firsthand experience observing original-thought theft, over 72 percent said they had indeed seen it take place. Reassuringly, the percentage of times it was called out, either on the spot or reported afterward, was 10 percent higher than incidents when the perpetrator was *not* called out on it.

HAVE YOU WITNESSED A MALE COLLEAGUE TRY TO PASS OFF A WOMAN'S IDEA AS HIS OWN?

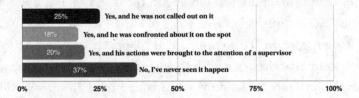

25%	Yes, and he was not called out on it
18%	Yes, and he was confronted about it on the spot
20%	Yes, and his actions were brought to the attention of a supervisor
37%	No, I've never seen it happen

0%   25%   50%   75%   100%

THE MOST VULNERABLE

Kate White, legendary editor in chief of *Cosmopolitan*, says that if you're a good idea person, you need to be extra vigilant in anticipating theftosterone and warding it off before it happens. "I came up the ranks as an idea person. And let me tell you, those who are not idea people often steal your ideas out of desperation. There are two ways to protect against that. Whenever possible, put ideas in writing and cc people. If your boss wants you to generate ideas in meetings, use a claim-the-floor strategy. You can say something like 'If I could have everyone's attention, I'd like to take a moment to provide some vital information that I think you will all find eye-opening and of tremendous value.' Don't just blurt out something like 'Maybe we should employ that strategy in California too.' It might get lost in the back-and-forth and then someone (probably a guy) will bring it up five minutes later as their own. Instead, gain the floor, and say, 'I have an idea. I think we should consider employing this strategy in California, and let me offer some research that explains why.' Don't start with all the research. Women tend to show their homework first."

BLOCKING THE PUNCH

But what if the theftosterone has already been perpetrated? What is there to do? Here are three possible courses of action:

1. **Amplification:** This requires the cooperation and involvement of women colleagues. Juliet Eilperin, a reporter for the *Washington Post*, spoke with women who worked in the Obama administration who had devised an antidote to theftosterone. It's a technique they called "amplification." Here's how it works. If a woman in a meeting makes a suggestion or presents an idea, another woman immediately acknowledges it, repeats it, and gives her credit. This shuts down any possibility that a man in the meeting can later stake claim to the idea for himself. The plan was executed with so much success that women in the administration noticed that Obama began calling on women in meetings more often.

2. **Claiming Affirmation:** If assembling a team of female support isn't possible for "amplification," and you're forced to go it alone, it's up to you to speak up. The lines you should have in your back pocket are "I'm glad you agree with the point I just made" or "It's so gratifying to get your affirmation of my suggestion from a moment ago."

3. **Male Advocates:** Women would benefit from a more equitable enforcement of communication justice. This requires that men also be on high alert for the appropriation of women's ideas at work. When they spot it, they can say, "That sounds exactly like what Kristin said just a few minutes ago. Do you have anything more that you could add to that?" or "I'm glad to see that you're aligned with the idea Kristin shared a little earlier."

BALANCING GENDER COMMUNICATION

Unlike imitation, theftosterone is not the sincerest form of flattery. It is what its title suggests: an unjust appropriation of a woman's voice. Given how long men have been engaging in this behavior, the prospect of eliminating or even dramatically curtailing these aggressions seems remote. For years the struggle to be properly respected seemed to be solely a battle for women to fight, and when they elected to go to the mat, often the consequences of being labeled militant or "nasty" outweighed the benefits. Men need to recognize the role they can and must play in combating this scourge to bring about more equity in communication in the workplace.

MORE ORDER IN THE COURT

Thanks to the Jacobi and Schweers study cited above, the Supreme Court's chief justice, John Roberts, has made changes to the rules governing the way the justices communicate during oral arguments. Now justices are allowed to ask questions individually, in order of seniority, after lawyers presenting in front of the court are finished. Sotomayor says the changes have made "an enormous impact," although Roberts still finds it necessary to intervene on behalf of interrupted justices three times as often as he once did. But in Sotomayor's eyes, the raised awareness has contributed to an attitude shift. "I found that my colleagues are much more sensitive than they were before. You'll see us, even now, when we're speaking, a judge will say, 'I'm sorry, did I interrupt you?'" Sotomayor said, adding: "That did not happen as much before."

The success of Roberts's intervention clearly indicates that men can make a difference in moving the needle. I know that in business meetings I attend, I try to be very conscious of respecting the input of women, especially those in more junior roles. It's vital to go beyond just not-interrupting to indeed validating points that are made and complimenting suggestions that truly add value. If I say something that is related to what a woman said earlier, I make certain to preface my thought with "I really like the point you made earlier. Another thing that came to mind on that topic is . . ." I find it ironic that men don't do this more, since it demonstrates a self-confidence and sense of security to be able to give credit to others for smart contributions. Julia Boorstin sees this as a key component to alleviating this problem. "Men so frequently don't realize that their comments are insensitive or uneducated. The more men can be aware of how they might be talking to women differently than their male counterparts, the better."

Why is this important in the context of workplace communications? Because the only way to be memorable and make an impact is to be heard. To be subjected to any of the aggressions we've discussed is a form a corporate muzzling that creates unnecessary anxiety for women, as they try to use their communication skills to stand out and be noticed. In short, it can be a confidence-killer that discourages women from speaking up, resulting in not just a stunting of the professional growth of women, but the stagnation of the companies they represent.

DO THIS	NOT THAT
Validate Others' Ideas	Appropriate Others' Ideas
Hold Your Thought Until Others Finish	Assume What You Have to Say Is Better
Acknowledge the Value of a Woman's Point of View	Condescend to Female Colleagues by Mansplaining
Accept That Great Ideas Can Come from Anywhere	Assume You Have a Monopoly on Wisdom

PART VI

TACKLING THE TECH CHALLENGE

Throughout history, some of the most significant technological innovations have directly impacted how we communicate. From the telephone, to the internet, to generative
AI, our skills as public speakers have become increasingly
reliant on our ability to navigate the latest tech tools. While
each of these tools has been designed to enable and enhance
our communication, technology also threatens to diminish
the role we all play, and in doing so, strip us of our individ-
uality. In the following chapters, we will strategize how to
not lose a sense of humanity and ensure that what makes us
distinctive in how we communicate still shines through.

12

POWERPOINT-LESS

"Now cover your right eye and tell me if you can read the bottom line of my husband's PowerPoint slide."

Admit it! Sitting through most corporate slide presentations is the bane of our professional existences. If they ever remake the film *A Clockwork Orange*, they could adapt the story to have the character of Alex get strapped to a chair and be forced to watch bone-dry, excruciatingly boring corporate presentations, in an effort to reform him from ever doing it himself again.

Anecdotally, there seems to be a growing aversion to presenting to an audience in person, especially among teenagers. In one reported case, a top student with a 95 percent grade average told her teacher she would rather receive a zero on her final than present it to her classmates.

People feel anxious when they have to give presentations and weary when they have to watch them.

In the business world, it's hard to find a practice that is so collectively practiced and yet so universally loathed as the slide presentation. In 2019, an *Inc.* magazine headline blared "Harvard Just Discovered That PowerPoint Is Worse Than Useless: Intuitively, anecdotally, and scientifically, PowerPoint may be the worst business tool ever created."

There is no shortage of smart business leaders who have called Power-Point's effectiveness into question. Jeff Bezos, when he was at the helm of Amazon, banned PowerPoint from meetings, saying in a 2023 *Inc.* article, "The problem with PowerPoint is it's easy for the author and hard for the audience."

It's designed to persuade, to get others to feel—*not* to get them to think.

"It's kind of a sales tool," Bezos said. "And internally the *last* thing you want to do is sell. . . . You're truth seeking. You're trying to find truth."

Bezos replaced slide decks with a six-page memo that he gives everyone thirty minutes to read at the beginning of a meeting. If people have questions, they can jot them down in the margins for later discussion. More times than not, according to Bezos, most of their questions were answered by the time he finished reading the memo. What this approach does is circumvent an executive from interrupting the presenter with a question that will be answered in the next few slides. Just imagine: the line "Yeah, I'm going to get to that in a minute" would be rendered unnecessary. But eradicating PowerPoint stands about as much chance as email going away. Most of us are mired in a corporate culture that relies on it as much as politicians depend on making speeches.

My beef, unlike Bezos, isn't so much with the tool itself, whether it be PowerPoint, Apple's Keynote, or any other slide deck application. Used with creativity and imagination, they can significantly enhance the storytelling elements of a presentation. These tools used to their full capacity can even bring a cinematic feel to how you share information. My objection is how badly underutilized they are, and at times even misused. As a result, I'm thankful when clients come in and freely admit, "I have no idea of how to put a deck together. Where do I start?" This allows us to teach good PowerPoint hygiene right from the start, instead of having to break old bad habits.

PASS ON KARAOKE NIGHT

The first golden rule is to not confuse text boxes on slides with presenter's notes. The worst thing you can do is put a full narrative script on the slide and then start reading, or what I call "slide karaoke." There is no quicker way to forfeit the engagement of the audience than to narrate your deck. The unforgiving reality of presenting is, the more text you have on the slides, the less your audience will listen to you, because people do not read and listen at the same time. I'd rather you be the star of the show, instead of being in a supporting role to some piece of software.

COMPLEMENT, DON'T REPEAT

Think of you and your deck as a sports broadcast team. The deck is the play-by-play person. You, as presenter, are the color commentator. The role of the play-by-play person is to provide the basic, foundational facts, which is the equivalent of what appears on the slide. After that call of the play, it's the color commentator's turn to speak, providing insights, perspective, and context. It's a complementary relationship. Now, imagine if after the call of the play, the color commentator came on and said the exact same thing the play-by-play person said. The redundancy of that would be intolerable. Well, that's the equivalent of reading your slides. When I find myself trapped, sitting through a PowerPoint narration session (I won't even call it a presentation), my first thought is, "Perhaps it would have saved everyone a lot of time had you just emailed the deck. I'm not sure why I need to be sitting here listening to you voice it over."

Our survey showed that nearly half the respondents over-rely on the text on the slide, answering that they either treat the words on-screen as they would their presenters' notes or stick very closely to the text that is written in full sentences. Less than 15 percent said they were comfortable having just one word or one number on-screen with an image for the background.

WHICH BEST DESCRIBES HOW YOU INTERACT WITH YOUR SLIDES?

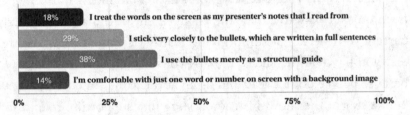

PROVOCATIVE OVER POLISHED

Spoon-feeding your audience with information that's presented in a style that's too predictable can work against you in your quest to be memorable. When everything looks the same and feels the same from slide to slide, nothing stands out.

According to the *Harvard Business Review*, getting your information into the explicit memory of your audience hinges on making your audience work. The more thought-provoking you are, the more you make the audience think, the more likely they are to remember what you told them. Conversely, eliminating all the rough edges (the illusion of spontaneous thoughtfulness) from your presentation in favor of extreme polish may make your content less sticky, for the simple reason that your audience can lean back and absorb your information more passively.

PICTURE THIS . . .

In an ideal world, presenters would make their slides almost entirely image-based, filled with some visual metaphor that parallels the point to be made. That's because pictures have retention superpowers that spoken words or printed text can't match. Yet most of the PowerPoint decks I see are built on a plain white background. That's a wasted opportunity. The image holds the power to establish the thematic backdrop for the message you want to convey. In the past, coming up with just the right photo could be a painstaking process that wasn't worth the enormous time invested to unearth just the right one. But today, a number of generative AI platforms make it possible to create a tailor-made image solely based on the text prompts you feed into their models.

Perhaps all that was needed in making images more accessible was a new and easier way, because the will to do it seems to be there. Our survey shows that nearly twice as many people said they use images for slide backgrounds "sometimes" or "frequently" as the number of people who responded "never" or "rarely."

IF YOUR PRESENTATION HAS SLIDES, HOW OFTEN DO YOU USE IMAGES AS A BACKGROUND?

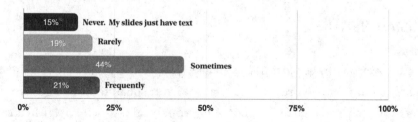

Presenting the information visually taps into a phenomenon called the picture superiority effect, which establishes that we are more likely to remember images than words. The theory, proposed by Canadian psychologist Allan Paivio in the 1970s, suggests that pictures provide a substantial benefit in three areas that are crucial to public speakers: engagement, understanding, and retention. It's an uphill battle to get people to understand something they don't find interesting, and if they don't understand it, good luck trying to get them to remember it.

Paivio discovered something that most of us have come to appreciate: Images capture attention more effectively than text. They can stimulate interest and emotional responses, leading to better engagement.

Another key aspect to the picture superiority effect deals with understanding. Pictures are critical because they often provide context that enhances comprehension. Paivio's studies show they can create associations and emotional connections that facilitate memory recall.

His theories suggest that there are two ways we store information in our brains: visually and verbally. Speaking to an image-free deck means that you are capitalizing on only one of the two retention tools—the verbal. Why forfeit a golden opportunity to benefit from the dynamic duo of memorability? When people absorb both images *and* words, they generally retain a higher percentage of the visual information over time. This is what he referred to as the dual coding theory, which leads to richer memory encoding and easier retrieval.

IMAGINE THIS . . .

But even if images are not available, you as the presenter can create some with your words. It's crucial that you speak to your audience in a way that they can visualize what you're saying. This is guidance I give in my one-on-one coaching sessions, sharing the information in a way that allows me to practice what I preach. "Imagine there are two distinct buckets," I say, "that represent differing communication styles. One over here [said gesturing with my left hand outstretched] is a vague, abstract and theoretical mode. The other [now gesturing with my right hand distanced from the other] is a style that is specific,

visual, and anecdotal." For instance, when I work with people to eliminate filler words from their delivery, I ask them to imagine that their
brain and their mouth are two cars on the road. "Think of your brain as
the lead car. It's about six hundred milliseconds ahead of your mouth,
which is the trail car. In that lead-car position, your brain is constantly
coming up to these junctures where it's deciding what road do I want to
go down and what words do I want to use to articulate that thought."

LOCATION, LOCATION, LOCATION

This technique is called the "method of loci," a technique that numerous
studies have shown improves memory. It's based on the theory that over
the course of millions of years, human beings have developed an ability
to remember information presented as a spatial relationship, meaning
the way in which objects are positioned in relation to one another.

Let's say you want your audience to remember a dramatic rise in
your company's growth since you implemented a new strategy. Before,
the growth rate was 3 percent, and now it's 39 percent. You could put
just those two numbers on a slide and reasonably assume that some
members of your audience will remember that data. But if you put the
3 percent figure over an image of a pitcher's mound and the 39 percent
over a photo of a mountain, you will dramatically increase the likelihood that people will remember how lopsided those two numbers are.

HONEY, I SHRUNK THE FONT SIZE

As the cartoon at the beginning of this chapter suggests, viewing someone's presentation deck shouldn't feel like you're being fitted for new
eyeglasses. Nearly every client deck I see in coaching sessions suffers
from two text-related problems:

1. There's just too much damn text.
2. To fit everything on the slide, the font size is reduced to single-digit.

To effectively address problem number one, be your own most brutal editor. Sit back and ask yourself, "Do I really need all this text?" Your mantra should be, "Just because I'm going to be saying it, doesn't mean people have to be seeing it." Remember, this is a complementary relationship, not a redundant one. Your slides are also not the place for you to display your prose-writing abilities. Full, grammatically complete sentences that resemble something you'd read in a book have no place in your deck. They should be swapped out for sentence fragments, snippets of information. For instance, take this slide headline:

"The W&E sector is a large and growing market which provides services to a wide variety of waste generators (e.g., from residential solid waste to nuclear materials). Certain subsectors of the industry are highly regulated and require specialized technologies/processes, providing significant barriers to entry."

Scale it back to just the essentials. You can verbally fill in any gaps that have been created: "A large and growing market | Highly regulated subsectors | Significant barriers of entry."

It's easier on the eyes and now you're no longer competing with your own deck for the audience's attention. Even something seemingly succinct can be given a haircut to make it more appealing. Something like "We adhere to a differentiated investment approach geared to deliver uncorrelated returns in all market environments" could be whittled down to: "Uncorrelated returns in all market environments."

Another effective way to dial back on the density of your content is to stop playing defense. Don't construct your deck to include everything, plus the kitchen sink, out of fear that someone in the room will call you out for having not included something. Remember, you are the expert on the topic you're presenting. If someone asks you why an element is missing from your deck, don't apologize. Instead, establish that for the sake of brevity, not everything was showcased in the deck, but that you're happy to address it now, in the Q&A.

PLAY WITH A FULL DECK

My point of view on how many slides should be in a deck has evolved over the years. Back in the day, if a client told me they had forty-five slides, my initial reaction was, "Whoa, that's *way* too many." I'd strongly suggest they find a way to trim the deck down to twelve to fifteen slides, not realizing of course that instead of making difficult choices on what content to leave out, people just crammed every inch of real estate on a dozen slides with the same amount of content. By doing this, not only are you creating a dizzying density to the look of your slides, but you are also bogging down the pacing of the presentation. There's not much point taking an hourlong presentation and shoehorning it into fifteen slides if you're going to be spending four minutes on each slide. All decks are different, but a good rule to follow is less than one minute of talking per slide. Flipping through your slides at a healthy clip will give a boost of energy to your presentation. But as I have stressed throughout, bring variation to everything you do. Try not to fall into predictable patterns where every slide is roughly the same length. Breaking up patterns and disrupting your own flow before your audience has a chance to get bored is a strategy you should think of as a proactive necessity, because as we established earlier, people get bored after approximately ten minutes. It doesn't matter whether it's in a classroom or a boardroom.

That's pretty discouraging news given how rarely our presentations are that short. You can avoid having your audience lose focus by inserting something different every three or four minutes. That could be a video or audio clip or a quick quiz or questionnaire. I'm always looking for ways to inject some fun and levity into the presentation, so I've created a game called What's Wrong or Right with This Prezzy? in which I show four video clips and ask the audience for their critique.

Challenge yourself to find a way to mix things up and change the flow of your presentation, because neuroscientists have found it's the best way to reengage a person's attention when it begins to falter. If you have special elements for your presentation, make sure not to cluster them too close together. Strategically space them out, every three or four minutes if you can, so that you don't fall into the ten-minute attention sinkhole.

SIZE MATTERS

The single-digit-font syndrome also strikes when we present charts and graphs. Ironically, the two most important pieces of information are written in the smallest possible font: what the X and Y axis of the graph represent, and what the different colors representing the lines on the graph signify. I would be okay with that if the presenter was vigilant about explaining both of those in their remarks, but it's rare that they do. Those identifiers are too tiny to read because when the presenter created their deck on a computer, they were likely three feet from the screen. That text didn't require squinting to read. But in a conference room, with the deck projected onto a flat screen, your closest audience member is likely ten to fifteen feet away. And although the screen itself is bigger than the one on your computer, the text still looks like the bottom line of that eye chart. Without providing that crucial information, pie charts and graphs are reduced to multicolored wheels and squiggly lines that leave your audience scratching their heads.

SYNC THE SENSES

If you want to maximize your audience's engagement and retention, you must never let their eyes and their ears fall out of sync. That means you need to be constantly mindful of speaking to what they are viewing at that very moment. Presenters who reveal all the information on a slide all at once run the risk of having the audience's eyes wander to the text at the bottom of the slide while you're elaborating on information at the top. That kind of sensory disconnect is a strong headwind to you being heard.

So, let's say you have a slide that is divided into quadrants. In the upper-left corner is a graph showing your company's performance four years ago. The upper-right quadrant has the same type of data from three years ago, lower left from two years ago, and lower right shows last year's figures. Most people display that slide with all four quadrants visible right away, which makes it much harder to corral people's visual focus. I hear the same complaint from executives when they distribute a printed deck to a handful of people sitting across a conference table. They're covering the content on page one, but everyone else is demonstrating PowerPoint impatience, flipping ahead to the last two pages in search of some conclusion. You would be far better off sending the deck to the attendees in advance of the meeting (the jargon equivalent is a "send-ahead") or distributing one after (a "leave-behind").

The most effective way to present your four-corners slide is to create builds or reveals, in which only one quadrant is visible when the slide comes up. Fully speak to it and then click to reveal the next quadrant, and so on. This gives you a fighting chance to keep the audience's eyes and ears from falling out of sync. But just to make sure that doesn't happen, use an imperative tone when drawing attention to something specific on the slide, rather than an optional tone. That means opting *not* to say, "Now, if we look at the quarterly revenue from a growth perspective since the acquisition, here's what we see . . ." In the phrasing of that, why even raise the specter that they might *not* look at the slide? After all, you are technically giving them that option. Try giving them a direct order instead: "Look at our revenue growth! Look at how it jumped after the acquisition!" This will bring more conviction to your delivery and direct more audience eyeballs to where you need them.

CONFORMITY MAKES YOU FORGETTABLE

Another slight wording adjustment that makes a surprisingly big difference in the sound of conviction in your voice is retiring the rhetorical question in favor of the declarative statement. Before presenters reveal a proposed solution or strategy, it's all too common for them to pose a question: "So how are we going to navigate through this challenge?" Now, you may be wondering, "What's wrong with that? I hear that all the time." You just answered your own question. If you hear it all the time, then I don't want you saying it. Don't be common. Don't be a conformist. Conformity makes you forgettable.

Break the mold! Take that rhetorical question and convert it into a declarative statement: "Now, here's how we overcome this!" This seemingly insignificant swap out brings more certainty to your voice and makes everyone in the room see you in the light of a visionary who's got a plan. Don't undermine your perceived confidence with another form of rhetorical question that has taken our culture by storm. It's an annoying verbal tic that is living rent-free at the end of our sentences and very few of us are even aware of its presence. It's the mindless habit of concluding our thoughts by saying, "Right?" It's rapidly become the Americans' equivalent to the Canadians' "Eh?" The reason this scourge is a problem is that confident people don't feel the need to be reassured after every sentence that they were heard and understood. People with gravitas don't obsessively seek validation. You're more likely to earn buy-in for your ideas by stating them with conviction than by asking people for it.

SLIDE ARCHITECTURE

There is no shortage of theories circulating as to how a slide should be built. We subscribe to what we call the "SAVE Your Slides" approach, SAVE standing for

Sparse

And

Visually

Engaging

To ensure that your deck is visually engaging, your first slide-building consideration should be "What's the visual here? What arresting imagery complements the ideas I want to express in this slide?" To achieve that minimalist, sparse look, embrace the 3–5 rule: No more than three bullets per slide and no more than five words per bullet. This might sound impossible to some of you, but a less-is-more mentality is a sensibility you can incrementally adjust to. Besides, there's never been anything wrong with leaving people wanting a little more.

DON'T DELEGATE, ELEVATE

For many executives, the slide deck is mistakenly an afterthought, an obligatory appendage to their communication efforts. It's an unwanted responsibility that frequently is handed off to someone on the communications or marketing team with little or no input from the executives themselves on how it should be built. What I hope you take away from this chapter is an appreciation for the return on investment you get by working to master this medium. A well-conceived, clear, and concise deck is a great reflection on your professionalism and enhances your executive presence because truly experienced executives usually possess enough self-confidence not to overtalk. The SAVE Your Slides strategy is also a show of respect to your colleagues, or whoever may be in your audience, that you value their time too much to regurgitate every factoid and data point at your disposal onto a slide and leave them to figure it all out.

To do this, you need to know the technology behind slide presentations. I urge you to not delegate this creative task, but rather elevate your deck-making abilities. If you really want to use your communication skills to separate yourself from the pack of your colleagues or industry peers, you must know how to wow your audience with a distinctive slide show that looks and feels different from the standard, drab, run-of-the-mill presentation. That means taking yourself to your nearest Apple Store on a Saturday morning and signing up for a free class on how to use Keynote, their presentation software, or find a similar tutorial Microsoft offers for PowerPoint. Understand how they work. See how professionals outside your industry establish a tech aesthetic that enhances their storytelling skills. And when you bring a few new tricks up your sleeve back to your company's marketing or communications team, offer to brainstorm and collaborate with them on a new template for your next presentation and all future ones. Seeing this as a creative opportunity rather than a tedious chore can lead to a better experience for your audience. That brings us back to the key public-speaking equation: the more enjoyable and interesting your presentation is, the better engagement you generate among your audience, the more engagement you create, and the more memorable your message becomes.

DO THIS	NOT THAT
Paraphrase the Slide's Information	Read Your Bullets Verbatim
Keep Slides Sparse and Visually Engaging	Turn Your Slides into an Eye Chart
Dictate Where on the Slide the Audience Is Looking	Allow the Eyes and the Ears of the Audience to Fall Out of Sync
Take Ownership of Deck Creation	Delegate PowerPoint to a Subordinate

13

ZOOMGENICS

YOU CAN READ A ROOM,
BUT YOU CAN'T READ A ZOOM

"Everyone in favor of Barry remaining on mute for the rest of the meeting,
raise your virtual hands."

In March 2020, COVID sent the whole planet into instant upheaval. Among the countless ripple effects was a massive distortion of our communication norms. Prior to that, Zoom, for most people, was something you made a car do when you floored the accelerator. But overnight, it became the only gear that could move our personal and professional communication forward.

For many, this new challenge was daunting. How do I present my best self in this strange new reality? The toxic new communications cocktail we all had to gulp down several times a day consisted of two parts conference call awkwardness, one-part cringey self-consciousness (from having to watch yourself) shaken together with a variety of tech challenges. No wonder virtual communication left many of us reaching for a real cocktail at the end of the workday. Our survey results support the theory that, if given the choice, a majority of people would opt for presenting in person rather than by virtual call.

HOW WOULD YOU COMPARE YOUR COMFORT LEVEL PRESENTING VIRTUALLY VS. IN PERSON?

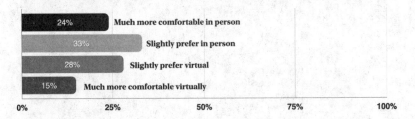

Another factor many of us were not ready for was the lopsided fatigue factor associated with virtual meetings. Who could blame any of us for underestimating this? After all, subtract the wear and tear of the daily commute to the office and shouldn't we all have felt a new lease on work life? This disparity between the levels of our energy, attentiveness, and mood during in-person meetings and virtual meetings was validated in a study in the journal *Scientific Reports*. In the study, researchers, who were part of an Austrian-funded project called "Technostress in Organizations," evaluated the responses of thirty-five students from a university who were attending lectures on engineering. Half the class attended the fifty-minute lecture via videoconference in a nearby lab and a face-to-face lecture the following week, while the other half attended first in person, then online.

Fatigue levels and mood were measured two ways. Students were monitored with electroencephalogram (EEG) and electrocardiogram (ECG) instruments that recorded electrical activity in the brain and their heart rhythms. They also responded to questions in a survey. The researchers' findings?

"Notable" differences were discovered between the in-person and online students, with fatigue growing for the videoconference students, who struggled to pay attention and complained of feeling tired, drowsy, and "fed up." By contrast, the in-person groups reported feeling livelier, happier, and more active.

While "Zoom fatigue" came to be acknowledged over the course of the pandemic as a legitimate phenomenon, I gradually became aware of another ramification of all-Zoomgenics, all the time. This is a lesser-known by-product that to my knowledge has not been studied at all, yet it is no less debilitating.

I call it "Zoom-nesia," the decreased ability to effectively differentiate between one Zoom meeting and another. Over the course of several months, I discovered an alarming trend: the details of these many virtual meetings were starting to merge together in my mind. I found my ability to recall specifics from any given meeting much more difficult. When I looked at this analytically, and asked myself what was different that could be causing this, it started to make sense. My setting for all these meetings was identical. Every day, I sat in the same chair, at the same desk, staring into the same computer screen. No opportunities to differentiate there! Now add to that the lack of variance in how the meeting's other participants show up (they're all in the same little square boxes) and you have a scarcity of audio and visual cues that help trigger our memories.

During the pandemic of 2020, health care workers discovered this very same phenomenon and decided to conduct a study. To examine a potential memory deficit for health information provided through telehealth, they presented older and younger adults with instructions on how to use two medical devices. One set of instructions was presented in person, and the other through telehealth. Participants were asked to recall the instructions immediately after the session, and again after a one-week delay. Overall, the number of details recalled was significantly lower when instructions were provided by telehealth, both immediately after the session and after a one-week delay.

To neutralize Zoom-nesia, I began taking notes during these meetings that were more detailed than ever before, right down to visual descriptions of the other participants. When in-person meetings returned, along with all the sensory landmarks that help our brains distinguish one experience from another, so did the precision of my memory.

Zoom fatigue and Zoom-nesia are just two factors that make it more difficult for us to project an air of confidence in virtual meetings. Other sources of distraction we rarely had to contemplate before include "How's my lighting? "Is my background an asset or a liability?" "Does my framing enhance my executive presence?" "With my close-up, how close is too close?" "How do I establish that all-important eye contact in this virtual dynamic?" Very few of us had access to a crash course on effective virtual meeting strategies before a familiar, comfortable approach settled into our daily routine. Several other considerations that public speakers need to contend with virtually that don't come into play in person range from managing the technology, to seeing (or not seeing) the bored faces of your audience, to the unsettling nature of seeing yourself constantly. Our survey indicated that all of the above are factors:

WHAT MAKES YOU MOST UNCOMFORTABLE ABOUT PRESENTING VIRTUALLY?

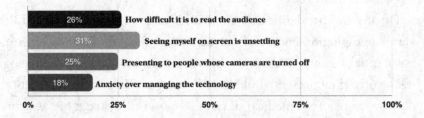

26%	How difficult it is to read the audience
31%	Seeing myself on screen is unsettling
25%	Presenting to people whose cameras are turned off
18%	Anxiety over managing the technology

0%   25%   50%   75%   100%

Although the frequency of virtual engagements has declined—to many people's delight—the importance of getting it right has not. It's interesting to me that many will invest significant attention and resources to having a professional photographer take a high-quality headshot for their profile picture, only to accept substandard results for their video meetings. This is a crucial mistake.

YOUR EXECUTIVE PRESENCE CHECKLIST

For the better part of two and a half years, I conducted over one thousand communication trainings over Zoom, Teams, or Google Meet. During that time, a handful of key factors emerged as essential to a well-executed virtual experience. Careful attention to a simple four-point checklist can boost your executive presence and enhance your stature.

1. The Setting

Keep in mind that the others in your virtual meeting are not just looking at you. They're taking in a host of other visual cues that are visible all around you. These inform their assessment of your polish and professionalism. But how many people actually give their Zoomgenics sufficient consideration? According to our survey, not nearly enough. The number of respondents who answered "Not very attentive" was 33 percent higher than those who replied "I pay attention to every detail."

HOW ATTENTIVE ARE YOU TO THE FRAMING, POSITIONING, AND LIGHTING OF YOUR VIRTUAL PICTURE?

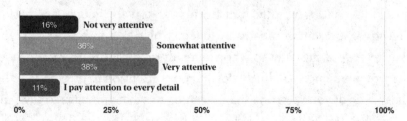

If you were hosting a dinner party for work colleagues in your home, you would likely make sure that your place was neat and orderly. For

better or worse, a virtual meeting is akin to that. You are inviting people into your home, and what they see says a lot about you. I wish I
could say that an unmade bed in the background was the worst of what
I've seen. Higher on the list of unmentionables are the dirty dishes on
the kitchen counter, the pile of laundry on the floor, and the cat's litter
box in the frame of the shot. Thankfully, the cat did not need to use it
during the call, but it certainly could have. Of all the first impressions
you want to make, that's not one of them.

Try to get some depth in the shot behind you. If you're backed up
against a wall, that will be the figurative, subliminal message you send.
A blank white wall is even worse. That's what kidnappers use to shoot
hostage videos. The only thing missing is holding up that day's news-
paper as proof of life.

A big window behind you might seem like a good idea on how to
achieve depth. In the majority of cases, it's not. As a rule, you don't
want the brightest spot on the screen to be in the background because
the webcam will adjust its iris to a more closed position and make your
face dark. Your face should be brightly lit, which is why O-ring lights
became such a popular accessory. If you wear glasses, though, be careful with reflections. The light from the O-ring can bounce off your
lenses and make you look like a crazed cyborg.

Bookshelves are a popular background, but unless they're ten feet
or more behind you, problems can arise. If the shelves are too close,
others can be distracted by any number of things: the titles of the books
you read (and your reading list reveals a lot about you), family photos,
and knickknacks or souvenirs from your travels. People are natural
detectives, present company included, which is a nice way of saying
they're nosy. If the clues to who you really are rest just over your shoulder, your audience will likely devote more attention to piecing together
the puzzle of your persona than listening to what you have to say. Anything that serves as a source of curiosity or distraction behind you is
blunting the impact of your message.

If you have no choice but to do a virtual meeting in a crowded office, make sure you flag those seated behind you, so they know not to do anything distractingly dramatic, like get into a shouting match with a colleague. At home, do your best to keep small children and pets on the other side of a securely locked door. I'm fortunate to have a well-behaved, eighty-five-pound German shepherd named Buzzy who is content to sleep on a sofa right next to me (but out of sight) until the meeting is over. Allowing your virtual call setting to be Grand Central Terminal can humanize your meeting in a charming way, but more often it leads to the kind of chaos you do not need.

Virtual backgrounds can be an effective way to neutralize messy or overly busy surroundings, but not all virtual backgrounds are created equal. Whatever you do, don't opt for the windswept, tropical beach. It only makes everyone on the call lament that they're on this call and not splashing in the waves and savoring a fancy tequila cocktail with an umbrella in it. Virtual backgrounds that display an ultrasleek and superluxurious thousand-square-foot living room probably aren't a good idea either. If you're pitching business and the prospective client thinks that that is really your home, they will inevitably come to the damaging conclusion that your rates are too high if that's the kind of place you can afford.

There are times, however, when flaunting a background can be a sound strategic decision. Recently I had to do remote training sessions while on a work trip to London, where for the past six years my firm has been working to build a base of clients. Thanks to the beneficence of the hotel at which I regularly stay, I was upgraded to a room with a fairly substantial terrace that had a great scenic overlook of Mayfair. In this case, I knew that the U.S. clients on the call would realize that my background was real and would inquire into my whereabouts. That would open the door in a less salesy way to let them know that London is a market that we service monthly, should they have any needs there.

One of the major drawbacks of virtual backgrounds is the weird "ghosting" that can occur, that phenomenon where too much movement of your hands and arms can make them eerily disappear. It also creates a strange glow around your silhouette that can make you look radioactive. I have discovered that the more light you have on your face and upper torso, the less you experience ghosting. I sit at a desk facing a floor-to-ceiling window with a directional desk lamp I point at myself. So far, I've been spared any unwanted disappearing acts.

At the outset of COVID, in anticipation of a Zoom-only work life, I went to the Clarity offices in the Flatiron District of Manhattan and took a series of photos that could serve as an ideal backdrop to virtual meetings. What could be better, I thought, than to bring my real world into the virtual realm. I took the pictures in landscape proportions rather than portrait because that's what best fills a Zoom/Teams screen. Then I experimented with another technique that proved effective. I took the picture slightly out of focus. This created what photographers call "depth of field," making the distant bookcase seem even more realistic. If I were actually sitting ten feet in front of the bookcase, there's no way that the backdrop and I could both be in focus. The other benefit to implementing depth of field? It fixes the attention of your audience squarely on you. It has worked surprisingly well. The majority of people I virtually meet with are shocked to learn that my background is not real.

Another option to elevate your game on virtual is to invest in a green screen, a large cloth backdrop (yes, it's actually a shamrock green) onto which you can digitally superimpose any image you want. Local TV weather forecasters have been using these for years to show maps.

A couple of notable benefits to going the green-screen route are that it reduces ghosting and makes it easy to have your company logo on a plain but colorful background behind you.

2. The Framing

If you've ever noticed the disparity between the portraits that are photographed by an amateur versus a professional, one of the first things that jumps out at you is the framing of the shot. Most people on virtual calls are way too close to the webcam. If I can see the pores of your skin, it's probably time to back off. Sit or stand approximately four feet away from your webcam. You should not be able to reach out with an extended arm and touch your computer screen. This will result in the proper framing: the middle of your torso at the bottom of the screen and the top of your head at the top.

Sitting too close to the webcam can also result in your lips being the only things that move in the shot. With that framing, even if you speak with your hands, no one can see them, so the movement is wasted. But if you back off three or four feet and you keep your elbows on the armrests of your chair, your hands can be in a resting position higher, just below your collarbone. That will place them in the lower third of the frame. From there you can speak with your hands and have the gesticulation to add movement and punctuation to your thoughts.

If you have a standing desk, take full advantage of it. Standing for your virtual presentations will always allow you to inject more energy and enthusiasm into your delivery. If you make the decision not to sit, just be mindful that the flow of adrenaline in your body can make it difficult to stand still and avoid rocking and swaying. Standing with your weight forward on the balls of your feet can prevent too much fidgety movement.

Another benefit to a wider framing is the ability to reference notes less conspicuously. When you're seated too close to the webcam, the disparity in your eyeline between looking into the webcam and looking down at your screen to read notes is accentuated. It becomes more obvious that you're reading instead of speaking. If you sit farther away, however, glancing down at your script becomes far less noticeable. In the early days of the pandemic, many of the guests on cable news shows leaned heavily on having detailed notes prompting them through answers to interview questions. When they sat too close to their computers, the problem was worse than just not making eye contact with the webcam. In some instances, you could see their eyes moving left to right in a reading motion, which shattered any illusion of natural, spontaneous conversation.

In many respects, videoconferencing (VC) allowed us to slip into bad habits. Many people seemed to think that VC stood for virtually clothed, focusing only on what they were wearing from the chest up. Sporting sweats and pajamas from the waist down is not a good way to try to get buy-in for your proposal, and it's certainly not how you go about impressing and instilling trust in a client. Environmental psychologists say that if you are underdressed, you are much more likely to underperform. But the habit that is proving particularly hard to break is using the cheat sheet that's been right there on our screens for the last two to three years. It's past time we ween ourselves off that crutch because when we're standing in front of a group of people in a conference room, those notes are often not available to us.

In my experience, not only are people too close to their webcam, but they also sit too low in the frame. This is fine if you want to look like you're sitting at the kids' table at Thanksgiving, but it doesn't do much for your stature and executive presence. Angle your webcam so the top of your head is grazing the top of the screen in the shot. Too much headroom (the space between your head and the top of the frame) diminishes your perceived authority. I've seen some people sitting so low, the lower half of their face is cut off by the bottom of the screen.

Your webcam should be exactly level with your eyes. This can be difficult, because if you have a laptop that is resting on top of a desk, the webcam will be too low and will shoot up at you. When these angles are dramatic, and you seem to be almost hovering over the webcam, we call this effect the "Paramedic's Pose," because I suspect that if I fainted on the street and regained consciousness, this is what I'd see: someone hovering over me checking my vital signs. If you see someone's ceiling in the background, that means their webcam is too low. Keep a couple of shoe boxes under your desk and use them to prop up your laptop. Conversely, a webcam that's positioned too high creates the wrong feel as well. This happens often when we're training clients in the financial industry who have monitors hanging above their desk. We call this effect the "Trading Floor Squat." By looking up at the others on the call at such a steep angle, you create a beseeching, subservient look.

3. The Sound

The audio quality of virtual calls is perhaps one of the most overlooked considerations. You can have a feature-film-caliber shot, but it's all going to waste if others can't make out what you're saying. Podcasts are popular in part because the audio has a rich, warm quality that creates an intimate feel. As a result, it's enjoyable to listen. To replicate this effect, find the room in your home or office that has the softest surfaces: rugs on the floor, curtains on the windows, furniture with upholstered fabric. You want as many soft surfaces as possible so that the sound gets absorbed. This year, I was in a hotel that had a wall of fabric instead of plaster in front of the desk in the room. The sound was so warm and so rich that the others on the virtual call asked if I was joining the meeting from a recording studio. The more intimate the sound of your voice, the more engaged your listeners will be.

For all these reasons, I continue to be amazed at how many people elect to do their virtual meetings from their kitchens. Sure, that six-burner Wolf stove next to the glass-paneled Sub-Zero refrigerator looks great in the background, but the kitchen is the worst possible place for a Zoom call. There are nothing but hard surfaces in kitchens, which makes the sound bounce all over the room, creating a hollow and tinny echo to your audio. Another setting that is not conducive to good audio quality is at the end of a long table in a conference room. Usually the webcam is part of the A/V equipment in the room and works robotically. While it may be good at automatically zooming in on whoever is talking, its audio quality is simply awful. Besides, sitting all the way at the end of the table, twenty feet from the microphone, is the antithesis of an intimate experience.

If you decide to take your virtual calls outside, just make sure it doesn't coincide with your neighbor's lawnmowing schedule. Outdoors should also be avoided if you happen to be in the landing pattern of a nearby airport.

Regardless of where you sit, investing in a good external microphone can upgrade the caliber of your call. Why wouldn't you want both the visual and audible experience on the call to be as pleasurable as possible for the others? The overall impression you leave others with is what counts, and the cumulative effect of all these smaller adjustments is a significant boost in your perceived executive presence.

4. Your Focus

Given the ubiquity of virtual meetings, there's been a cascade of advice on how to make your communication thrive in this new reality. But what is noticeably absent is one of the most important mindsets to adopt: not obsessing over a digitally distorted audience response. Even in the physical world, every audience has its fair share of zombies—lifeless ghouls giving you the death stare, sucking the life energy from you. If you've ever had that intimidating experience standing at the front of the room or onstage, you know what a confidence-killer it can be. In a virtual setting, you have to deal with "Zoombies," the other people on the call who make the in-person zombies seem like the life of the party. On Zoom, that unsettling feeling increases dramatically.

We often hear how crucial it is to "read the room." Is your audience engaged or are they starting to drift? Are they showing signs of impatience because you're not getting to the point quickly enough? Can you assess their interest level from their body language and facial expressions? Are more than the usual number checking their phones? In person, the ability to properly read these signs is an enormous asset.

But in a virtual-first world, we are stripped of this ability. I have concluded that while you might be able to successfully read a room, you cannot read a Zoom. In fact, attempting to do so could undermine you and hurt your delivery. There are several reasons why trying to read a Zoom may be more of a hindrance than a help.

In person, when your audience breaks eye contact, you can see what else has captured their attention. Perhaps they're handwriting notes, or following along with the printout of your deck. On virtual, we might immediately assume that they're looking down to text a friend or check their email. Our human nature is to assume the worst. In that little box, your attendees may appear distracted when they are, in fact, engaged.

In person, most of us feed off direct eye contact. It's what boosts our confidence that we are the center of attention and what we are saying is resonating. But on Zoom, we appear to our audience either well below or to the side of the webcam, so we never quite feel fully connected to those listening to us.

If you're presenting, chances are your audience is on mute, so don't count on getting a laugh or any other kind of audible reaction. Delivering a clever line that prompts the sound of crickets rather than chuckles can be unsettling.

Then there's the confidence-crushing trend of people turning off their cameras. This is the virtual equivalent of your audience getting up and leaving the room. Admit it. If this has happened to you during a virtual presentation, in the back of your mind you're wondering if they're even still listening.

We pay keen attention to all these signals for one simple reason: validation. We want to know with certainty that our presentation is hitting the mark and getting heard. But when the virtual dynamic deprives us of the cues we get from in-person meetings, we try too hard to read garbled signals, often to the point of distraction. The less affirmation we get, the more we want it. And the less we get it, the more our confidence suffers. Overly focusing on others' reactions can sap your focus on the most important thing: your own performance.

Here are some strategies that can keep you from trying too hard to read the Zoom.

- **Close the Windows**

It may sound completely counterintuitive, but close all the video windows that show your audience. This eliminates a debilitating source of distraction and frees up more mental bandwidth to concentrate on the articulation of your message. This tactic also improves your eye contact, which in a videoconference setting is straight into the webcam, not vertically down the right side of your screen, where your audience typically appears.

- **Drag the Thumbnails**

Another effective tactic is clicking on the top bar of the thumbnail chain of participants and dragging it from its default position vertically down the right side of the screen, to the very top, middle of the screen. There it will flatten out horizontally and the thumbnail of the person you're talking to will be no more than half an inch below the webcam, making eye contact easier.

- **Humanize the Webcam**

If you find it hard to keep your focus on that little green dot at the top of your laptop screen (or wherever your webcam might be), take a small photo of someone you feel comfortable talking to and punch a couple of holes just below their face. Then place the newly made holes directly over the webcam and secure the picture in place. Now you have someone to look at while you're talking.

- **Pin the Most Engaged**

Determine who is the most engaged audience member, and then "pin" their window so it is the only one that shows up. If you feel more comfortable having some member of the audience visible, then at least it should be someone who boosts your confidence. If you can't depend on any of the expected guests to be properly attentive, plant a colleague among the audience members and tell them to remember to nod and smile periodically.

For many of us, public speaking can feel like being out on a limb all alone. The virtual component can make that limb feel even more shaky when we're overly attentive to visual cues that aren't reliable. For better or worse, we may have at least one foot in this Zoom world awhile longer. So, the more you can control the dynamic, rather than letting it control you, the more successful you are likely to be.

DO THIS	NOT THAT
Keep the Webcam at Eye Level	Have the Webcam Shoot Up at You
Sit Four Feet from the Webcam	Sit So Close That Only Your Head Is Visible
Create Some Depth in Your Background	Sit in Front of a Plain White Wall
Look into the Webcam Frequently	Have Your Eyes Look All Around

14

COMMUNICATING IN THE AGE OF AI

"Jeremy, you were a strong a candidate, but we're giving the job to this avatar who always has the perfect answers and never asks for a day off."

The best thing about my role as a communications coach is that I get to help people improve a skill that's vital to their success and happiness. Sometimes it involves overcoming a deep anxiety over public speaking and helping them be more confident. The second-best thing is the chance to work with amazing, first-of-their-kind companies that are doing extraordinary things in their quest to solve complex problems. After a day of training with these innovators, I often leave humbled and in awe of the advancements that are being made at warp speed. But nothing matches the feeling of having my mind completely blown the way it was after working recently with a company called HeyGen.

Through generative AI technology, HeyGen can create a completely realistic avatar from just a minute or two of real video and audio of you speaking to the camera. The idea is to allow busy executives to be in two places at one time. While they're boarding a flight to head off to a conference, their team back at the office can be feeding a script into the HeyGen software that will allow the executive (or their avatar) to deliver a streaming video message to the entire company—with no costly production crew, no scheduling issues, no flubbed takes. The tone of voice perfectly replicates the executive's, as does the lip sync. But that wasn't what floored me. I had seen reports out of China that showed this digital duplication of real people was already taking place. What made my jaw drop was what happened when HeyGen's founder, Joshua Xu, clicked a translation button and transformed an English-speaking salesperson appearing in a video into a presenter who was communicating in fluent, perfect Italian. For every executive who has stared at their calendar in search of a sliver of white space that never seems to be there, this is as close as you can get to putting a clone of yourself to work.

Up to that point, I knew that AI would change the way we communicate, but it wasn't until I saw that demo that I fully realized how dramatic that impact is likely to be. But this rapidly advancing capability seems to be on a collision course with people's desire for their leaders to demonstrate authenticity. One will need to yield to the other at some point. For the sake of doubling productivity in a chief executive, are we willing to be spoken to by a reasonable facsimile of the real person? If you think I'm nuts for even proposing this as a possibility, keep in mind that we human beings have a terrible propensity for forfeiting some of our freedoms, and a big portion of our personal privacy, for the sake of convenience, productivity, and being part of something trendy.

Many of the communication experts I've spoken to in researching this book express reservations over this murky merging of real, authentic communication and something spit out by AI. Among those concerned is Jay Carney. "People are already overwhelmed. It's hard to get their attention now. They're going to doubt with good reason whether what they're hearing is actually the real person. I think that there's a lot of risk there. It makes it even more important for communicators to focus on authentic voice messaging that can defy AI."

Great communication begins with connection, as Oprah Winfrey likes to say, and connection is a human activity. But more and more, the role of communicator is being assumed by automation. Technology has had a role in the steady erosion of our verbal skills, which has led to our spoken communication muscles atrophying. When was the last time you called someone in their teens or twenties and actually had them pick up? We consistently hear from employers, teachers, and parents that young people's struggles with spoken communication are getting worse. As they have retreated deeper into their digital devices, letting their thumbs do the talking for them, anxiety levels over public speaking have spiked. It's only logical to assume that when these generations establish themselves as the leaders of tomorrow, they will be all too happy to abdicate the lion's share of communicating to AI tools.

We're already seeing the leading edge of this with job interviews, an area that has always been predicated on human interaction. A survey from Resume Builder released in 2023 found that by 2024, 40 percent of companies would utilize AI to conduct preliminary-round interviews with job candidates. Of those companies, 15 percent said hiring decisions would be made through automation, with humans staying out of the process. What does that mean for the value of social-emotional maturity when you're vying for a job? Will the technology be sophisticated enough to detect subtler soft social skills that will be in increasing demand as everything becomes more automated?

Given that the creation of presentation decks is considered the bane of many an executive's existence, the chances seem good that task will be delegated to AI. According to our survey, this is already happening. Given that mainstream use of AI technology is such a recent development, it was surprising to us that so many people are already utilizing it for this purpose.

DO YOU USE AI TO CREATE WORK PRESENTATIONS?

Instead of hours of work devoted to slide creation and far too much time wasted staring at a blank computer screen trying to figure out what to say, an executive (or their reports) can simply give a voice command and have the technology spit out a game plan in a matter of seconds. If you hate content creation, this is a dream come true.

This scenario presents both a challenge and an opportunity. The challenge is that more speeches and presentations are likely to resemble each other in a dry and automated style that fails to captivate. But when everything starts to sound the same, those who want to be distinctive will be forced further from the conformity zone and hopefully be inspired to bring a more imaginative and creative approach to how they communicate their message. In a future where originality is likely to suffer, the growing scarcity of it will make its value skyrocket, like any commodity.

Those responding to our survey were already aware that the best way to distinguish the way we communicate from machines in the future is by focusing on softer, human elements.

The nightmare scenario is to spend time writing content that others assume you delegated to ChatGPT. This is an opportunity that must be seized. Businesspeople need to capitalize on this opportunity to stand out from the multitudes who will surely abdicate the creation of their narrative to a machine. That means relying more heavily on the tactical devices we've examined in the preceding chapters that make

HOW DO YOU THINK AI WILL ALTER THE WAY WE COMMUNICATE IN THE FUTURE?

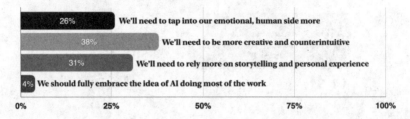

your communication memorable: deploying the Magnificent Seven, storytelling, humor, empathy, expressive body language, and manipulating your voice to be in a constant state of variance. No machine can do that, at least not yet. One of the most eloquent voices on this subject belongs to LinkedIn founder Reid Hoffman, who, despite being one of the founders of OpenAI, appreciates the abyss into which we are all staring. "All big, new technologies both have opportunity and threat, and in a sense, those are the great ones. I mean when cars were invented, people were scared of them. They regulated initially that someone had to walk in front of them waving a flag because who knows what would happen." (Terrific analogy driven by historical context with a splash of humor—an impressive and memorable cocktail.) He went on to say, "So, it's legitimate to think, what's the downside, what's the concern, and that's real. However, the opportunities are also great, and I think we have to say we need to navigate this the right way, but I think we can actually use AI to create more jobs, we can use it to help fight disease . . . there are a bunch of things that it can be instrumental to and we need to not lose sight of that."

Distinguishing ourselves as we compete with AI for the most memorable and captivating voice in the room may end up being a footrace. As technology becomes more and more sophisticated, we will need to be students of its capabilities. When we've assessed those, we should ask ourselves, "What is still outside AI's reach?" Then make those qualities, which remain in humans' sole possession, a cornerstone of how we connect with others through our communication. As daunting as this sounds, we human beings are likely to have more chances of standing out and being distinctive, but we're going to have to push ourselves harder than ever before to excel in those capabilities that, for now, remain distinctively human.

DISRUPTION DENIAL

In 2011, I got a call one day from a student at MIT who wanted my help. He was building an app that he said would help make people better public speakers and he wanted my input. Keep in mind, back then AI was nothing more than a Stanley Kubrick/Steven Spielberg movie, so I'm only slightly embarrassed to report that I told him I didn't think a machine could ever do what I do—words that I and countless others have eaten over the past dozen years. Fast-forward to today and there are numerous AI tools that can help you communicate better.

I even wound up providing message development and media training for the founders of one such company when they were in incubation stage. I remember saying to the founder, "You realize in giving you the power to articulate the value of what you bring, I'm probably putting myself out of business someday." We laughed at the irony, but ultimately we worked together and developed a collaborative relationship. Today our firm uses AI tools strategically to help improve people's communication skills, tools that measure the speed of your voice, the filler words you say, as well as the weak and repetitive words you use. AI will even recommend how to be more concise. But this apparent encroachment on our turf has been invaluable because it has inspired us to reexamine what it is we bring to speech coaching that AI cannot. Machines, at present, cannot coax out of you an engaging story and help you craft it and weave it expertly through a speech or presentation. If you ask AI to come up with a metaphor and analogy, what you get is something hopelessly clunky. Humor, clever transitions, tools to heighten your executive presence and display conviction in the way you speak, all of those are currently out of the reach of generative AI.

CORPORATE OZEMPIC

In 2024, *Fortune* did an article on artificial intelligence's impact on jobs in the tech sector. The headline was so clever that I've often cited it in Clarity's training sessions as a great example of a creative label and analogy all rolled into one. The story was titled "Corporate Ozempic," claiming that companies were getting "thin" in their employment ranks thanks to the growing capabilities of AI, but none of them is willing to admit that that is how they're slimming down. No large language model (LLM) could have likely come up with that memorable line.

The awareness that this human–machine collaboration is what yields the best results is gaining more and more support from the most prominent people in tech, among them Daniel Ek, the founder and CEO of Spotify.

"I often think the toughest part of communicating is the blank page—that first draft. AI models have really helped break down those barriers to get started. In my work, LLMs have made it so much easier for me to ask questions on an infinite range of topics and be more purposeful about what I'm trying to say. However, though I think tools like these are incredibly important to how we'll all communicate going forward, I don't believe that AI alone will net you the best results. For me, it's the combination of people and machines that will together drive the future of human communication."

I like to think of AI as a lump of clay and a potter's wheel, the raw materials for making functional pottery. But without the hands of a person bringing a distinctive artistic flair to it, what you get is a bowl or vase that looks like millions of other bowls and vases. It's up to the person at the wheel to bring the finesse and flair that make the finished product distinctive.

As an experiment to illustrate the point I just made, I asked ChatGPT to start a chapter of a book that examines the future impact AI will have on human communication. This is what it came up with:

"Artificial Intelligence (AI) is poised to revolutionize human communication in ways that are both profound and unprecedented. As AI technologies become increasingly sophisticated, they are beginning to influence the way we interact with each other, from natural language processing tools that enhance our ability to communicate across languages and cultures, to AI-driven content creation platforms that are transforming how we produce and consume information. These advancements are not merely augmenting human communication; they are reshaping it by introducing new forms of interaction, enabling more personalized and context-aware communication, and potentially altering the very nature of how we connect and collaborate."

While it touches the bases you would expect it to, there's nothing distinctive or memorable in that opening paragraph to pull you in. It's all very high-level and broad-strokes. To offer what AI cannot, and captivate an audience, we need to be more specific, more visual, more anecdotal. Over the past twenty-plus years, that has consistently been the quest in coaching others to be more memorable presenters. But now there's a new sense of urgency we should feel in making that stylistic transition. The future of communication and the need to cut through all the noise and clutter in order to be memorable could very well be "survival of the pithiest."

CONCLUSION

When you take a step back and look at the big picture of all the guidance in this book, you may notice that the advice closely resembles the wise counsel we often receive in our daily lives:

1. Push beyond your comfort zone.
2. Stand out rather than blend in.
3. Break the mold of traditions.
4. Develop an allergy to conformity.

If you've come this far with me on the ride, you clearly take your communication skills seriously. I urge you to keep this book within arm's reach at work or at home (or both!) and refer back to it when you are preparing for a meeting, client pitch, keynote speech, or presentation. I want you to feel you have a private coach at your side at all times, providing answers to any and all questions that arise, because under the watchful eye of an experienced coach, you can't help but get better.

As we have discussed, there is no better way to display to others your executive presence and leadership abilities than to dazzle them with polished public-speaking skills. Professionally, it is the outer skin we all wear that carries outsize importance in creating that crucial first impression. From there you can use your ever-growing communication prowess to reinforce and validate those positive impressions. Regardless of your background, the extent of your education, or the depth of your work experience, the ability to express yourself articulately and memorably can be one of the great equalizers.

In our careers, we always want to be projecting progress, advancement, and self-improvement. Any hint of professional stagnation is not an option. What better way to showcase your own evolution than to demonstrate constantly improving public-speaking skills? Use the tools in this book to up your game every time you speak. As with any talent in which you're looking to gain proficiency, determined reinforcement of good habits and tireless practice are essential. Think of how you would approach the pursuit of excellence if you were a professional tennis player. You wouldn't go out onto the practice court and just slug ground strokes with a sparring partner for an hour or two. That would be the equivalent of going through your presentation once or twice while sitting at your desk. Pros looking to boost their ranking in the world take it much further. They work for hours on their first serve, their second serve, their volleys at net, their drop shots, their overhead smashes, their passing shots, etc. Approach your preparation and rehearsal very much the same way. This book has outlined all the components to your communications game in the hopes that you will give each one proper attention:

- Crafting a cohesive narrative
- Using storytelling as a primary vehicle
- Creating a couple of memorable lines using the tools of the Magnificent Seven
- Breaking free from slide karaoke
- Cultivating a warm demeanor
- Using your voice like a musical instrument
- Employing a strategy for your body language

When you achieve an elevated level of execution in all these individual areas, the whole becomes greater than the sum of the parts—and that's when you dazzle people. We discussed earlier the powerful feeling that comes over people when the body releases endorphins. That's what happens when you ace a presentation. The brain equates that with your having overcome a high-stakes challenge, emerging victorious. Once you view the experience as rewarding, the body is not only flooded with the feel-good hormones, endorphins and dopamine, but it reduces the release of cortisol, the stress hormone. I've seen this physiological response transform many a reluctant public speaker into someone who never wants their time in front of an audience to end.

Embracing the work needed to get *really* good at this fuels the public-speaking virtuous cycle. The more you prep and practice, the better you get. The better you get, the greater the chance you'll captivate your audience. The more they're captivated, the more you enjoy it. The more you enjoy it, the more you'll say yes to invitations to do more. The more you do, the better you get and the more memorable you become, and around and around it goes. This centrifugal force will propel your stature, your reputation, and your career forward in unimaginable ways. Now that you have the toolkit, all you have to do is get to it!

ACKNOWLEDGMENTS

Speak, Memorably would not have happened without the generous support of many people. First, our thanks go out to Wayne Kabak, a man who is unequaled in generously sharing his wisdom and intellect.

A special thanks to Hollis Heimbouch and Rachel Kambury at HarperCollins, who exhibited unbounded enthusiasm for this project from our very first meeting. Their warmth, encouragement, and expert guidance made the writing process a delight.

Writing this book while keeping our day jobs was possible thanks only to the hard work and professionalism of the entire team at Clarity Media Group. Our chief operating officer, Mariko Takahashi, exhibited her characteristically calm leadership, which freed us up to coach clients by day and write by night. Her wise input throughout the entire process was invaluable. Clarity's executive director of training services, Chelsea LoBue, worked her creative magic in crafting and styling the look of all the surveys in this book. The only reason this balancing act of work and writing maintained its equilibrium is because our chief of staff, Hannah Gross, has the best organizational skills on the planet. She expertly carved out time and space for the writing process, while making sure all our clients felt fully cared for. Together with Abby Kohn and Lindsay McMullen, this team's amazing support is a big reason why the project finished on time.

Promoting a book is a daunting challenge, in some ways even more than writing it. But the entire team at Fortier Public Relations was relentlessly diligent in devising a great plan and executing it. Thanks to Mark, Adam, Marcus, and the rest of the team.

The decision to create homemade cartoons for the beginning of each chapter made it necessary to find a talented illustrator who could capture the *New Yorker* style we were looking for. Alexis Seabrook did a tremendous job and was an absolute delight to work with.

Phil Siegel was incredibly diligent and thorough in his vetting of all things legal. Unsolicited, he checked in with us throughout the process to see how things were going.

The experiences we drew upon from thousands of training sessions were a result of the kindness and generosity of those who helped grow our business over the past twenty-five years. The following, in alphabetical order, have transcended the status of client, and are regarded at Clarity as benefactors and friends of our work family:

Audrey Adlam, Michelle Alban, Shara Alexander, Rachel Allgood, Laura Arrillaga-Andreessen, Suzy Berkowitz, Cindi Berger, Julia Boorstin, Julian Boulding, Jarryd Boyd, Mike Brady, Teresa Brady, Chris Buck, Katherine Burns, Maggie Carr, Rachel Carr, Gregor Cattanach, Lucy Cherkasets, Alex Cohen, Jamie Cooper, Chantelle Darby, Sunil Desai, Rimjhim Dey, Peter Donald, Jeannine Dowling, Amanda Duckworth, Daniel Ek, Sheila Feren-Thurston, Lizzie Fishman, Randi Friedman, Jonathan Gallen, Sean Garrett, Jason Ghassemi, Kelsey Grady, Adam Grant, Rajaa Grar, Maire Griffin, Judy Grossman, Desiree Gruber, Rebecca Hahn, Liesl Henderson, Susan Henderson, Reid Hoffman, Vojtech Horna, Jennifer Hyman, Kristen Jones Connell, Stephanie Jones, Alexander Jutkowitz, Liz Kaplow, K.C. Kavanagh, Bryce Keane, Darcy Keller, Jennifer Khoury, Andrew Kovacs, Stephanie Kozinski, Slawomir Krupa, Jessica Kurdali, Elizabeth Linder, Linda Lipman, Zsoka McDonald, Shan-Lyn Ma, Caryn Marooney, Sally Marvin, Sandi Mendelson, Jessica Merz, Veronica Miele Beard, Natalie Miyake, Vidhya Murugesan, Paul Olsewski, Suzi Owens, Jen Psaki, Jennifer Robinson, Stephanie Ruhle, Sheryl Sandberg, Anthony Sanzio, Elisa Schreiber, Amanda Schumacher, Nell Scovell, Kerry Sulkowicz, M.D., Bethridge Toovell, Sheila Tran, Loretta Ucelli, Jonathan Wald, Angela Watts, Margit Wennmachers, Kate White, and Tamika Young.

Like most writers, we relied heavily on a few select haunts to retreat to for brainstorming sessions. In New York City, EJ's Luncheonette on

Third Avenue was the place that always welcomed us with open arms and hot tea and coffee. Mahmud, Kazi, and Islam were the kings of hospitality there. True to the name of her establishment, Jean from Caffeine in Westhampton Beach kept us well caffeinated in the warmest and most welcoming way imaginable. Across the pond, in London, Stuart Procter's amazing team at The Beaumont created a home-away-from-home that made writing a joy.

During a project like this, it's vital to have people around who ground you and remind you of the important things in life. Leland Stein wielded his immense charm to keep us laughing and happy through the entire process.

ABOUT THE AUTHORS

BILL McGOWAN, founder and CEO of Clarity Media Group, is a two-time Emmy Award–winning journalist and the bestselling author of *Pitch Perfect: How to Say It Right the First Time, Every Time.* He is the top global communications adviser to the leading names in business, tech, entertainment, AI, sports, fashion, cybersecurity, beauty, media, and finance. He has coached the founders of Amazon, Meta, Twitter, LinkedIn, Instagram, Spotify, Snapchat, and Airbnb, as well as Oscar, Emmy, and Grammy winners and World Series, Super Bowl, and Olympic champions.

JULIANA SILVA is a communications coach for Clarity Media Group and an opinion columnist at CNN.com. At Clarity, she works across all industries in the U.S., Latin America, and Europe to prepare C-suite executives and their teams to deliver memorable and engaging interviews and presentations in multiple languages. As a trainer, she draws on her extensive digital and broadcast reporting experience, providing trusted communications counsel to firms like L'Oréal, VISA Latin America, Comcast, LinkedIn, Wells Fargo, TikTok, Rosewood Hotels, Google, and Bacardi.